In this landmark work, Dr. Sherice Janaye Nelson shatters decades of silence to reveal the extraordinary yet overlooked impact of Black women in the Congressional Black Caucus. Through groundbreaking research, she exposes how these remarkable leaders wielded their "radical imagination" to reshape American democracy, even as they faced the crushing weight of both racism and sexism.

*Visibly Invisible: The Black Women of the Congressional Black Caucus* charts an electrifying journey from Shirley Chisholm's historic arrival to today's powerhouse legislators, documenting how these fierce pioneers transformed grassroots activism into revolutionary policy. Nelson masterfully captures their political brilliance—showing how they navigated the shadows of a system designed to exclude them, yet still managed to champion transformative change for both racial justice and gender equality.

This tour de force is far more than just another political history—it's an urgent rewriting of the American democratic story. Essential for scholars of politics, civil rights, and gender studies, Nelson's work stands as both a triumph of historical recovery and a rallying cry for the future. By finally bringing these hidden figures into the light, she reveals not just what was accomplished against staggering odds, but what remains possible in the ongoing fight for true democracy.

Caroline Heldman, PhD, Professor of Political Science
Occidental College

Many social scientists compose research to "fill in a gap" in the literature to which they claim to be an expert. They aspire to enlighten society about something not addressed in existential research or to convey something erroneously discussed more accurately. But how does one fill in the gap when the gap is a chasm? The interplay of racism and sexism, which are interwoven into every aspect of American life, make any discussion of Black women in government a monumental task to address, where most only provide toothless theories evinced by obtuse statistics. It takes a once-in-a-century scholar to tackle the chasm of the work and legislative achievements of the women of the Congressional Black Caucus (CBC) in context and with historical accuracy. I guess that makes Dr. Sherice Janaye Nelson a once-in-a-century scholar!

In *Visibly Invisible: The Black Women of the Congressional Black Caucus*, Dr. Nelson, without question and for the ease of the reader, charts more than 50 years of the intersectional journey of Black women in the highest legislative chamber in the country. Dr. Nelson manages to do this without glossing over any of the women, acknowledging the more well-known characters like Shirley Chisholm while simultaneously spotlighting those whom history often neglects, such as Corrine Brown. Visibly Invisible will be the benchmark for manuscripts that attempt to mark the path of any race-gender demographic in government institutions because while it discusses the systemic oppression often faced by racial and gender minorities, it also transcends the stereotypical conversations of oppression and focuses on the successes and triumphs without performing revisionist history!

Timothy E. Lewis, PhD, Associate Professor of Political
Science Southern Illinois University, Edwardsville

# VISIBLY INVISIBLE

VISIBLY INVISIBLE: THE BLACK WOMEN OF THE CONGRESSIONAL BLACK CAUCUS

Copyright © 2025 by Universal Write Publications, LLC

Library of Congress Control Number: 2025901241

ISBN: 978-1-942774-46-4

Printed in the United States of America.

Mailing/Submissions:

Universal Write Publications, LLC
421 8th avenue, Suite 86
New York, NY 10116

Website: UWPBooks.com

Book Cover Design: Lance Harris
Contact: LanceHarrisDesign@gmail.com

This book has been partially supported with a financial grant from SAGE Publishing.

# VISIBLY INVISIBLE: THE BLACK WOMEN OF THE CONGRESSIONAL BLACK CAUCUS

Dr. Sherice Janaye Nelson

Universal Write Publications, LLC

New York, NY

I dedicate this book to all the unnamed Black women

who fight to bring light into dark places:

Remember that the light ALWAYS wins!

# Table of Contents

# *Foreword*

## Ann-Marie Waterman

Fifteen years pass very quickly when you are associated with a brilliant, sophisticated, thought leader like Sherice Janaye Nelson, PhD. As her former mentor, now colleague and friend, I have witnessed firsthand a conscientious master's student blossom into a powerhouse political scientist, analyst, speaker, administrator, and associate professor. This scholar, only educated at Historical Black Colleges or Universities (HBCUs), is passionate about Black people and their politics. This is evidenced by how she has chosen to invest her time and her talent: Director, Alabama Agricultural & Mechanical University, Master of Public Administration Program; Board member, Metropolitan Baton Rouge Chapter of the National Coalition of 100 Black Women, Inc.; Board member, Dillard University, Center for Racial Justice; just to name a few places where she utilizes her skills and abilities. This author is committed to disrupting the field of political science by producing scholarly work, which establishes new theories that inform the audience about Black power in action.

Thus, it was no surprise that her first work, *The Congressional Black Caucus: Fifty Years of Fighting for Equality* (2022), would prepare our Black political palates for her next book with a framework to understand how the Congressional Black Caucus (CBC) was formed, developed, and evolved. It was a natural output of her scholarly work as a Black Diasporic researcher who is constantly evaluating how Blackness is treated in democracies. The initial text highlighted not only the accomplishments achieved, or the challenges the CBC faced, but rather explained their maneuvers and strategy in political context to demonstrate they were not playing checkers with "one step forward and two steps back." Rather, they were engaged in a game of multidimensional chess that required carefully positioning of political muscle and moral conscience to achieve the crowning glory of inclusive democracy. Dr. Nelson showed us how the original 13 members of the CBC bore the burden of carrying the weight of the entire Black race's legislative burdens on their backs as well as serving their respective constituents' needs. The broad strokes of *Fifty Years of Fighting* prepared the perfect canvas to focus our attention on the details of the metaphoric supporting characters of the Black legislative scene.

In this Dr. Nelson's timely and important second book of the duology, *Visibly Invisible: The Black Women of the Congressional Black Caucus*, we are refreshingly exposed to the secret sauce, or maybe the women are more aptly described as the mysterious, invisible characters that use their special resources of activism, community participation, and desire for better communities to produce the legislative gifts of humane rights for women, children, and other marginalized populations. The gifts of these women would manifest themselves in the form of better education, wages, and welfare for marginalized people, in general, and Black people in particular. Dr. Nelson shows us how the women of the CBC served as essential cogs, assisting in producing power to move the wheels of the Black legislatures as the caucus generated productive outcomes.

Actually, the timeliness and the importance of this text could not have aligned more seamlessly with the 2025 national state of affairs. This book is a perfect compendium of information to aid any reader who wants to get meaning and understanding of the nation's current and potential future legislative circumstances. The current circumstances are a result of systemic barriers that are keenly constructed to disenfranchise those who are not White males. Thus, the work's historical march through different eras in American politics centering these Black women is powerful. This lens allows Black women to hold space that the legislative body often refuses to seed. The lens will also help readers see similarities, from past to present, of how Black women have consistently been the invisible arbiter pushing American democracy: with little to no recognition.

Nevertheless, the power of the CBC is growing. In the 119th Congress, with Donald Trump serving as the 47th president, the CBC will boast its largest membership inside of the Congress with 62 lawmakers. Black women make history as two of them will sever in the Senate for the first time in American. What is certain is these Black female lawmakers will be serving during what has repeatedly been characterized by mainstream media as "hostile political times." What we have in this text is a roadmap, perhaps even recipe, to see how the previous female legislatures agitated for and contributed to the CBC preserving its role as "the conscience of the Congress."

If you want to experience and engage the invisible work and visible presence of the contributions of the women of the CBC, then reading *Visibly Invisible* is of great value. Dr. Nelson has poured her whole self into producing a readable, comprehensive gem showing us how a group of women dared to change the things they could not accept.

Ann-Marie Waterman, PhD

Chief of Staff, Coppin State University

Author, "Privatizing Education" in *Newschaser: The Rhetoric of Trump in Essays and Commentaries* (Harris, 2017)

# *Acknowledgments*

Writing a book is never a one person job! I want to start by thanking Dr. Ayo Sekai for her belief in me and her constant encouragement about this book project. Her insistence about the need for this work is why you the reader have this book today. Understanding how to capture all the women of the Congressional Black Caucus in one book was no easy feat. Yet, you consistently pushed me to be focused in my approach. I want to also thank Dr. Pearl Ford Dowe for writing what many Black women in political spaces have felt. Your work *The Radical Imagination of Black Women* provided the framework I desperately needed to situate this book and speak for generations of Black women.

To my colleagues Dr. Timothy E. Lewis and Dr. Caroline Heldman, thank you for your honest feedback and review of the book. Your commentary helped me to strengthen the work; consequently, my claim about Black women in the legislature cannot be refused or ignored in the academy. To Dr. Ann-Marie Waterman, thank you for reading the work and writing the foreword. Your support and my academic pursuits have persisted across decades and I am grateful to the scholars of the MacArthur Historical Black Colleges and Universities project: Dr. Erica Williams, Dr. Melanye Price, Dr. Sharlene Sinegal-DeCuir, Dr. K.T. Ewing, Dr. Illya Davis, Dr. Bertis English, Dr. Daniel Black, Dr. Darius Young, Dr. Jelani Favors, Dr. Elieen Kane, and Dr. David Canton: THANK YOU! Your comradery has helped me to never again question if I belong!

To my husband the Reverend Doctor John Kurtis Coar III, you are an indispensable force in my life. Thank you for always encouraging me to be the scholar God has called me to be! In this work you were my researcher; you gladly gathered bills and denoted historical trends when I needed it most. Your commitment to my success with this book has undoubtedly shown me your willingness to sacrifice. Thank you for finding a way to give me room while always being there when I need you most!

# INTRODUCTION

The Congressional Black Caucus (CBC) is the first racial caucus established in the U.S. legislature after the seminal Civil Rights Act of 1965. This Act helped to ensure the right to vote for many Blacks in the south who had been denied access due to racism. Although Blacks were serving in the House of Representatives before the caucus was founded in the spring of 1971, Black members understood that legislative cohesion was imperative if they were to maximize on the tenets of the Civil Rights Act of 1965. The founding 13 members were representatives from northern states but keenly understood that they were representing the interest of Black folks throughout the country. Twelve of their members were male with one lone female Shirley Chisholm of New York. She was the first Black woman to be elected after 195 years.

This burden and opportunity to speak of, advocate for, and legislate around the disparities in the lives of Blacks as citizens of the United States was and continues to be the mission of the caucus. CBC members understood that they were descriptive representatives, as well as symbolic representatives, responsible for substantive legislation. They understood the burden of being Black in America and could articulate this burden in legislative terms even if that legislation was not passed into law. They also understood they were a symbol of full Black citizenship in the American civil liberties and civil rights framework. Their election and creation of the Caucus symbolized the collapse of dual sovereignty, a sovereign system that allowed Blacks in southern states to be denied their full rights as citizens of the United States. Such a design purposely denied the interests of Blacks by legally designating them as property in the effort to deny congressional representation.

The history of Black citizenship in its duality and its subsequent denial is the cornerstone of the CBC. The formation of this Caucus allows Blacks to be represented through the citizenship provided in the 14th Amendment to the U.S. Constitution. This right of citizenship is symbolized by the creation of the first racial caucus as their legislative representation safeguards Blacks through the equal use of the social contract, a contract that theorizes that the state's responsibility is to protect its citizens in response to the adherence of established laws. Those laws are created by legislative representatives. However, a review of the evolution of Black citizenship in the United States shows that Blacks have lacked protection by the state due to their ambiguous citizenship status.

The CBC's formation represents the collapse of dual citizenship for Blacks throughout the country. The Civil Rights Acts of 1957, 1960, 1964, and 1965 were necessary to allow Blacks full access to their citizenship. The CBC organizing around the interest of Blacks, not only in the state they represented but also across the country, was needed by these northern political representatives. The protection of and the advancement of full Black citizenship has historically been the chief concern of the CBC. Their continuous presence in the legislature provides the safeguard intended by the social contract often making them the moral voice of the nation.

The active denial of citizenship for Blacks at the state and subsequent federal levels is due to constitutive racialism, which is used to establish the racial contract. Instead of adhering to the social contract, slave states along with free states decided to bar Blacks from citizenship at the founding of the country. This allowed for Blacks to be permanently ostracized from the federal political community as citizenship is first experienced at the state level. This is demonstrated by the state-issued birth certificates, identification cards, and marriage licenses. Exclusion from the political community could only be remedied by representation at the federal level. Access to this larger political community through the creation of the CBC denoted belonging and access for Blacks and their interest. Yet, full citizenship in the United States by way of the constitution for Blacks has been tenuous from the founding of the country, to the founding of this Caucus, to the present day.

In an effort to appear as they belonged the CBC decided to mirror the structure inside the House of Representatives. They organize themselves in a way that could not be disregarded. The Caucus' founding leadership understood that mirroring the structure of committees, subcommittees, and task forces would prepare their members to serve as effective chairmen and chairwomen once seniority was attained. It was a strategy that considered the longevity of the Caucus as a constant vehicle to represent the interest of Blacks. It is through the leadership of the chair that we see the Caucus evolve into a legislative force that has been duplicated by many other ethnic groups.

The development of the CBC over the last 50 years coincides with the increase in civil rights, civil liberties, and the visibility of Blacks and their issues throughout the country. A review of the Caucus also shows a growth in its female membership. Understanding that female expansion inside of the Caucus while firmly establishing the contributions of these women is the focus of this book. The work reviews the legislative accomplishments and the legislative influence these women had in different eras since the CBC's founding. The work covers the span of over 50 years to include every Black woman who served as a member of the CBC from the 93rd Congress to the 108th Congress. The goal was to chronicle each era through a historical frame that remembered the happenings of that time, while subsequently showing how these Black women used their legislative power to influence these historical moments in the country. The book will discuss the invisible work these women participated in, which propelled the legislative activism used by the CBC. It will also provide a political analysis rooted in their invisibleness in relationship to the larger legislative body. The work asserts that a racialized government structure filled with sexism and misogyny has made Black women very visible, while simultaneously making the work they do invisible.

After writing *The Congressional Black Caucus: Fifty Years of Fighting for Equality*, it was imperative to write a book solely about the women of this Caucus. The historical research showed that much of the hard work these women had and have done is being attributed to others at best and forgotten at worst. Finding a way to present their struggle as Black female legislators while respecting their different personalities and unique trials was daunting, until *The Radical Imagination of Black Women* (Ford, 2024), by fellow Howard alumnus, provided a framework for analysis. Her argument states that Black women's political ambition is unique as it manifests outside of formal politics. Activism, community participation, and its subsequent building of a better community are often the sources of Black women's ambition. This is seen in the legislation they sponsor, the floor speeches they make, and the ways that they engage in the mainstream media.

Their historic and continued commitment to improve the lives of the oppressed and forgotten throughout the United States articulates a radical vision for a full democracy. To paint this picture, the work engaged a plethora of sources. The original archival research at Howard University's Moorland-Spingarn Research Center produced over 400 pieces of archival materials. Most of this material was used in Chapter 1 of the book. The HistoryMakers was another key source due to the gaps in documentation and preservation of the Black American historical records. The founder Julieanna L. Richardson started interviews in 2000 at a time when there was only one large-scale methodic attempt to capture African American history, during the 20th century, from a first-person perspective. These interviews allowed for verification of written biographies and context often answering the question why. The Government Publishing Office has published a compilation of short biographies for each Black American who served the Congress in 2007 (Committee on House Administration of the U.S. House of Representatives, 2008). Since that time, they have updated that publication and digitized the information compiling those biographies from 1870 to 2022. Most of the biographical information found in this work comes from this source.

All legislation and subsequent legislative summaries were found at Congress.gov. This digital resource had every piece of legislation sponsored and passed by all the members of Congress. It was an invaluable source for creating a timeline that showed how these Black women sponsored legislation especially after crisis that deeply affected Black people. C-SPAN, which was created 8 years after the founding of the CBC, made it easy to evaluate the floor speeches made by these women and observe how they were received by their colleagues. This highlighted the importance of local news; many journalistic giants like *The New York Times*, *Washington Post*, and *The Los Angeles Times* were used. Yet, the impact many of these women had was often in local news close to or inside of the districts they served.

These Black women were visible in their communities, which in many ways feed their radical thought process. Yet, they were often invisible in the larger legislative structure. Such invisibility is connected to their intersecting oppression and the inability to see Black women as rational actors. The work forward this argument by doing a brief review of the CBC and why it was necessary in 1971. It discusses the need for Black legislators to be morally upright to gain respect in an effort to influence their colleagues, legislation, and the American people. The end of the chapter provides an example of such morality despite political party. Finally, Chapter 1 discusses rationality and the reasons why Black women are not seen as rational actors.

Chapter 2 introduces the foundational women of the CBC. The chapter opens with a review of the historical events, which happened in the judiciary that shaped their legislative era. It discusses the strategies each of these women used to be successful as legislators in spite of their extreme minority because of their race and gender. The chapter shows how these women used their radical imaginations to ascend to the House of Representatives through state legislatures. It also discusses key legislation that established them as a force to be considered, while establishing the foundation that other Black female legislators could build upon.

Chapter 3 discusses the expansion of the female members of the CBC and how that expansion furthered the consideration for the collective. Black women began to fill the ranks making them more visible and propose legislation that helps Blacks as a collective. They were also unafraid to propose legislation that directly affected Black women.. The chapter opens with a review of the legislative careers of Maxine Waters, Eleanor Holmes Norton, and Barbra Rose Collins. The longevity of their careers, while being the children of the civil rights struggle, shaped the expectations for the women who joined the Caucus after them.

Chapter 4 goes on to discuss southern expansion where southern states by using the Civil Rights Act of 1957 and 1965 saw a group of women becoming the first in their state to join the House of Representatives. The chapter continues with a discussion about Newt Gingrich and how his time as speaker changed the structure of the House of Representatives with the hope to discourage Blacks and in particular Black women. Yet, during this era two women entered the Congress as strong fighters for the Black collective: Shelia Jackson Lee and Barbara Lee. The chapter concludes with a discussion about the female legislators who entered during the Y2K era. These women foresaw how election normalcy was to change the lives of Americans, which ensured a greater shift for Blacks in their representative communities.

Chapter 5 brings the reader into the modern day discussing the growth of the CBC and the Obama Administration. The chapter discusses the CBC achieving political saliency. The women in combination with the male members were represented on all standing committees, giving them a power achieved only through seniority. The chapter discusses the women who continued to push the envelope in the House of Representatives and how some of the women in the Caucus formed a more progressive movement that challenged many of the forms first practiced by the Black Caucus. The chapter also discusses how the exit of female members has greater impact on different governmental spaces. The chapter closes with a discussion around respectability politics and the need for political sophistication as well as cultural connectivity.

Chapter 6 concludes the work with a review of the Black female senators who have all been members of the CBC. The chapter opens with a discussion about why there have been so few Black women to serve in the U.S. Senate by showing it is connected to the presidency. The chapter argues that the Senate is the gateway to the presidency and that Black women's intersecting oppressions make it difficult for the American psyche to cede that amount of power to a Black woman. The chapter also discusses the masculine nature of the presidency, which is duly ascribed to those who serve in the Senate. The chapter continues with a review of each of the three Black women who have served in the U.S. Senate and the legislation they sponsored. A review of a few of these women's floor speeches shows that they were unafraid of speaking their minds particularly around the issue of race and the preservation of democracy. The chapter closes with a brief discussion about the 2024 presidential election where Kamala Harris made history as the first Black woman to be the candidate for a major party. The chapter asserts that although radical in imagination, Black women are confounded by their intersecting oppression.

Chapter 7 affirms that Black women substantively, and over their time in Congress, sponsor more legislation than other race-gender groups. The chapter introduces a theoretical frame inclusive of research questions centered around the visibility and invisibility of these Black women. A review of key legislation sponsored and cosponsored by these Black women in proceeding chapters is coupled with a comprehensive evaluation of legislation sponsorship. Black women's immense sponsorship serves as an invisible action receiving little attention from their peers or the media yet leading to visible outcomes. This chapter uses quantitative data from the 93rd Congress to the 118th Congress to solidify the phenomenon of Black women sponsoring more bills than other gender–race groups. The chapter closes with a discussion about Black women's need to do and be more to be seen as rightful belonging legislators in the House of Representatives.

# CHAPTER 1

## A Historical Review of the Congressional Black Caucus

There is no possible compromise in the case of race, its social construction, and hierarchical manipulation as these factors were present during the country's founding. White elites at the founding understood the convergence of their interest revolved around the prevention of tyranny. Such prevention of White southern elites was wrapped in the diminutive legal status of Blacks. Although northern White elites did not agree without compulsion, they understood the importance of the young country's unification. A compromise was made in the best interest of White elites to allow poor Whites to feel privileged. Thus, White superiority became gospel. Such a gospel was in direct opposition to an American creed that stated that all men were created equal with inalienable rights.

Therefore, Blacks used the tenets of the social contract to push against this White gospel forming the CBC. The CBC is the result of the success of Blacks in the Civil Rights era of the 1950s and 1960s. They are the symbolic and literal representation of the collapse of the inequities perpetrated by southern Whites and accepted by northern Whites. Eleven of the original 13 CBC members were also members of the Democratic Select Committee, founded in January 1969, and represented districts in the north. Three of the thirteen were born in the southern states of South Carolina, Louisiana, and Georgia. Many of the other representatives were first-generation born outside of the south as their parents had migrated in their early adulthood. The same political barriers that prohibited Blacks to vote in the south were not as effective in the north, which allowed Blacks to coalesce around particular issues that translated into political power as discussed by Grant (2020, p. 312):

> Black elected officials could amplify the voices of Black Americans in ways that were not possible before the Great Migration unlocked their political potential. In other words, the Great Migration also created a class of legislators who had the ability to bring the concerns of the Black community onto agendas in state legislatures and in city councils.

From the city councils and state legislators, Black federal representatives emerged constructing the CBC.

The CBC's existence forced Whites to question how and why they had been societally deemed superior and calls the racial hierarchy into question. The question of their supreme morality and the idea that the Black race could occupy the same space of the "Honorable" is disconcerting. A Congressman or Congresswoman is addressed as the Honorable. This is the denotation that congressional representatives are the model of chief morality in our society along with judges. Such moral fortitudes are believed to be abnormal in the Black race as a racial hierarchy was established to solidify this idea in a societal structure. This social phenomenon is even more prevalent for Black women who suffer from a double-minority status, which expose intersecting oppression (Crenshaw, 1991). Yet, the lack of morality is based upon the savage identity assigned to Blacks in the name of commerce.

The CBC has used moral strategy to drive the inequities faced by everyday Black Americans. Their noble acts continually show them as the chief moralist as they decided to peacefully resist. A historical example is the CBC's boycotting of President Nixon's State of the Union address. The president's refusal to meet with them was the signal that the government was disinterested in the interests of its people. Blacks were getting closer to full citizenship in the United States, citizenship that had been structurally denied since the Compromise of 1877. Their protest aligned with the demands of the social contract, which the gospel of White superiority has continued to deny.

A more recent example of the CBC as the chief moralist was the press conference held in the summer of 2020 to introduce the George Floyd Policing Act. The summer of 2020 was wrought with turmoil; a global pandemic was raging, which in turn sparked controversial conversations about structural racism and the experiences of Black Americans. Yet, the state's violation of the social contract with the killing of George Floyd by asphyxiation punctuated the controversy. The untimely death of Floyd and the global outrage were seized by the CBC. The chairwomen of the Caucus, Karen Bass of California's 37th district, introduced police reform legislation that was passed in the House of Representatives in a matter of weeks (Nelson, 2022).

Black representation in Congress is a sign that the issues of Black Americans must be addressed even inside of a racialized government structure. A refusal to address Black interest calls into question the validity of the American democratic–republic in its entirety. The CBC's use of chief moralist as a strategy naturally garners attention by the free media. In many ways, this is purposeful as non-state-sponsored media is a limited tool used to ensure the health of a democracy. Although media conglomerates have participated in framing the issues of the American people, it is needed for the functionality in keeping the trichotomous system accountable to the people: even if through awareness alone.

The media's coverage of the discriminatory experiences of Black Americans often opens the CBC to examination and critique. In the case of Nixon's State of the Union boycott, the Caucus was viewed favorably as no suitable reason was provided to the Caucus as to why the president would not meet them. They were a newly formed group that represented the interest of people who had only gained full political rights 6 years ago. Their boycott highlights the recalcitrance of Nixon, which simultaneously exposed the morality of the CBC. The media attention garnered by this incident also signaled the CBC that the exploitation of the executive branch was where they could have early victories. However, that strategy shifted after the election of President Barack Obama.

The political leanings of any sitting president, indiscriminate of their political party, need to be monitored by congressional members as a function of the constitution. Thus, the CBC often used this strategy to seek support for Black interest inside of a racialized government structure designed to leave unaddressed the interest of Black people. The mighty 13, the founders of the CBC, knew that the political power they had was one of disruption. A newly formed racial caucus, which struck out against their own political party, inside of a body of 435 members, by design, cannot have institutional power. Yet, these legislative founders knew that they were preparing for a day they may never serve to see: the attainment of the political power to decentralize such political power in the House of Representatives. This power was attained in the 111th Congress, which encompassed the lame duck years of George W. Bush and the commencement of Barack Obama's first presidential term.

The historical resistance the CBC faced as a small racial caucus was still prevalent in the Obama years and persists today. Yet, the disruption strategy used by the mighty 13 couldn't be used by successive CBC generations. To best comprehend the shift in strategy, a review of the administrative organization of the Caucus is important to note. The Caucus appointed a chair and organized sustained committees, subcommittees, and task forces, which prepared them to serve as committee chairs and subcommittee chairs once tenure was secured in the House of Representatives. The mighty 13's conscious effort to organize this way showed how to structurally fight racism by first mimicking the structure. Their ability to successfully mimic the Congress within their own racial caucus is indirectly connected with the power they gained to decentralize power in Congress. Such decentralization helped produce a viable Black candidate for the presidency: Barack Obama.

"Party Factions in Congress" by Daniel DiSalvo articulates nine eras in the 20th century and the 21st century concerning Congressional intraparty factions. I contend that the Black Caucus establishes the 10th creating their own faction in 2009 during the 111th Congressional session based on DiSalvo's (2009, p. 31) definition of a faction as:

> a party subunit that has enough ideological consistency, organizational capacity, and temporal durability to influence policy making, the party's image, and the congressional balance of power. Factions exist when some party members share a common identity, are conscious of differences that separate them from other party members and vote collectively on a range of issues.

The CBC fit that description at the commencement of the Obama Administration because as a far-left voting bloc they have separated themselves from other Democratic Party members (Table 1.1). They articulated policies that often differed from the Democratic Party's platform, and Congressional tenure provided access to congressional power not available to the mighty 13. This power was defined by the CBC's consistency in voting behavior for over 40 years and saturation among the congressional committees. Such saturation required a shift in strategy that also required a permanent shift in the Caucus' use of the media.

Table 1.1    Extended 20th-Century Congressional Intraparty Factions

| | |
|---|---|
| 1. Old Guard—Conservative Republicans | 1896–1916 |
| 2. Progressives Republicans | 1904–1928 |
| 3. Populist Democrats | 1896–1924 |
| 4. Southern Democrats | 1938–1976 |
| 5. Liberal Republicans | 1938–1968 |
| 6. Liberal-Labor Democrats | 1958–1976 |
| 7. New Politics Democrats | 1966–1980 |
| 8. New Right Republicans | 1964–1996 |
| 9. New Democrats | 1986–2007 |
| 10. CBC Democrats | 2009–present |

In the 111th Congress, the CBC had 41 members. Of those members, four held positions in party leadership. James Clyburn of South Carolina's 6th district was the Democratic Whip. John Lewis of Georgia's 6th district was the Senior Chief Deputy Majority Whip. Maxine Waters of California's 43rd district along with G. K. Butterfield of North Carolina's 1st district were two of the eight Chief Majority Whips. Of the 17 leadership positions in the Democratic Party Congressional leadership, not including the Speaker and the Speaker's Assistant, CBC members held four of those positions. The CBC was represented on all standing committees, and three of their members chaired standing committees. Bennie Thompson of Mississippi's 2nd district chaired the Homeland Security Committee; John Conyers of Michigan's 14th district chaired the Judiciary Committee; and Edolphus Towns of New York's 10th district chaired the Oversight & Government Reform Committee. This power only grew in the 116th Congressional session.

The CBC entered the 116th Congress as the largest and most powerful Caucus in history to date, with 55 Members and 5 full Committee Chairs. Elijah Cummings of Maryland's 7th district chaired the Committee on Oversight and Government Reform. Eddie Bernice Johnson of Texas' 30th district chaired the Committee on Space, Science, and Technology. Robert "Bobby" Scott of Virginia's 3rd district chaired the Education and Labor Committee. Bennie Thompson of Mississippi's 2nd district continued to chair the Homeland Security Committee. Lastly, Maxine Waters of California's 43rd district chaired the Financial Services Committee. The "Big 5," as they were affectionately known, did not count the 28 CBC Members who served as Subcommittee Chairs in the 116th Congress.

Therefore, when Chairwoman Karen Bass presented legislation on police reform, the positionality of the Caucus had changed. The Caucus was still committed to their posture as the chief moralist in the House of Representatives, but the use of the media needed to be in concert with the political power the Caucus had amassed in its 49-year history. The Caucus' ability to decentralize power through the mimicking of the congressional structure resulted in a structural takeover delineated above. Such structural power required the CBC to use more acceptable political tools such as symbolism to substantiate them as the powerful legislators they had become. This resulted in a press conference that announced police reform with almost 9 min of silence.

Karen Bass, chairwoman of the CBC, organized legislators inside of the congressional building to kneel with African kente cloth for 8 min and 46 s. This was symbolic as it was the exact amount of time Derek Chauvin, a then Minneapolis police officer, kneeled on the neck of George Floyd. Met with a barrage of scrutiny for such a political symbol, Bass stated, "The significance of the kente cloth is our African heritage ... our origins and respecting our past ... and for those of you without that heritage who are acting in solidarity" (BBC News, 2020), Yet, the use of kente cloth as an ethnic symbol was not new, members of the CBC had worn kente cloth on other occasions, including an event that mark the 400th anniversary of the arrival of enslaved Africans to America and to the State of the Union address in 2018 during the Presidency of Donald Trump.

The ability of a Black woman, Karen Bass, to organize the Democratic Party leadership around African heritage as the leader of the CBC was something unthinkable to those who founded the Caucus. The ability to force mainstream media to recognize and discuss African heritage, normally reserved for graduation ceremonies of students in historically Black fraternities or sororities, was quite different than the attention the founding members garnered in the Nixon State of the Union Address boycott. Although criticized by many in mainstream media spaces, this display led by the CBC as the chief moralist was abundantly clear. The public execution of a Black man by an operative of the state was a violation of the social contract supposedly available to every American. Thus, the CBC's ability to draft comprehensive legislation, secure party leadership support, and pass the bill in 11 days amid a global pandemic spoke of their power as chief moralist.

The preparedness of the Caucus and the power they have amassed are connected to development of counter-strategies so that their existence would be impactful. Such development was implored when many of the founding members attended the First National Black Political Conference in Gary, Indiana, in 1972 (Poletika, 2019). Due to Black migration, the civil rights movement, and the Civil Rights Act of 1965, many northern industrial cities were seeing a rise in Black elected officials, and Richard Hatcher was among those officials becoming the first Black mayor in Gary, Indiana, in 1968. At this conference, there were throngs of Blacks with varying interests. Those interested organized themselves around two ideologies: one of integration and one of Black Nationalism. The assassinations of Malcom X on February 21, 1965, and of Dr. Martin Luther King Jr. on April 4, 1968, proved to many Blacks that integration was not the answer for Black liberation. Yet, Blacks had made political progress with the election of sitting officials at the local and now federal level with the CBC. This made finding a place for Blacks to meet in 1972 ostensible:

NBPC organizers, who had begun planning the conference in 1970, struggled to find a city willing to accommodate an influx of politically engaged Black Americans. Gary Mayor Richard G. Hatcher, an advocate of civil rights and minorities and one of the first African American mayors of a major U.S. city, volunteered his predominantly Black city. Not since the 1930s, with the first meeting of the National Negros Congress in Chicago, had such a massive and diverse gathering of people of color convened to advance their rights. Approximately 3,000 official delegates and 7,000 attendees from across the United States met at Gary's West Side High School from March 10 to March 12. (Poletika, 2019)

From this meeting, a Black Declaration of Independence was erected, a document that recognized that Blacks had not achieved full citizenship in the United States and outlined a blueprint for Black Independence in an internationalist model. An attendant reported to the *Indianapolis Recorder*, "Thousands of Black people left Gary energized and committed to making electoral politics a more relevant/meaningful exercise to promote Black interests" (Poletika, 2019). It was upon this energy that the CBC was determined to build.

The document has 12 provisions: (1) Jobs and Income; (2) Foreign Policy; (3) Education; (4) Housing and Urban Problems; (5) Health; (6) Minority Enterprise; (7) Drugs; (8) Penal Reform; (9) Democratic Administration Appointments; (10) Justice and Civil Rights; (11) Self-Determination for the District of Columbia; and (12) The U.S. Military. These have remained the focus of the Caucus throughout its 54-year history. The Caucus' first Chairman Charles Diggs is noted for saying, "Black people have no permanent friends, no permanent enemies ... just permanent interests" (United States House of Representatives, 1971). It is in this spirit that the Caucus still operates to date but has repositioned themselves as a powerful Caucus.

Many of the founding members understood that to tackle the aforementioned issues, far more information was needed to be amassed by those with expertise. Attendance at the First National Black Political Conference had made one thing clear for many of the founding members: The Caucus could not be everything to everybody. Therefore, they concerted their efforts into being the best legislators for minority and oppressed peoples' interests. To achieve this, resources were needed, and archival records show that a CBC Dinner Committee was organized in Washington, DC, on June 18, 1971, shortly after their founding in February 1971. The letter states, "Capable staff must be hired, vital research performed, local concerns responded to, and pertinent information disseminated throughout the nation if it is to be a viable leadership force" (Congressional Black Caucus Preliminary Inventory, 1971). It is from this fundraiser that the Annual Legislative Weekend that convenes in mid-September in Washington, DC, each year was conceptualized.

The Conference is the congealing of fundraising, social engagement, and legislative examination, making it the leading policy conference on issues affecting Blacks in the global community. The Annual Legislative Weekend was and still is the realization that Blacks have access to political power through elected representatives, representatives based upon the structure of denial, due to inferiority, who should not hold or have access to such power. Therefore, the weekend was and will continue to be a collision of two worlds, one that deems their existence superior and the existence of the other ephemeral. One world that will restructure, retool, strategize, and be intentional about their existence through demanding civil, political, and social rights for the least of these, and another world full of people who are committed to denying their existence. The Annual Legislative Weekend is organized each year in a daring fight for full access to the social contract that has been historically denied to Blacks. It is a world on the collision course with another world that depends on Black existence while simultaneously denying its power.

The salience of the CBC and its ability to effect change was felt well before they decentralized power in the 111th Congress. In 1994, 2 years into the Clinton Administration, the Republicans made great gains in the midterm elections. In the 103rd Congress, Republicans were the minority with only 176 seats, yet in the 104th Congress they gained 54 seats gaining a majority over Democrats who had 203 seats to Republicans' 230. The shellacking experienced by the Democratic Party ushered in a new Speaker of the House: Newt Gingrich, the representative from Georgia's 6th district, a district held in the 118th Congress by CBC member Lucy McBath. The Republican Party ran on a platform of smaller government. When Congressman Gingrich became the speaker, he brought about sweeping changes.

These changes were captured in a *New York Times* article by Michael Wines written on December 8, 1994, entitled, "Republicans seek Sweeping Changes in House Rules." The article explains how the Speaker intended to make government smaller by reducing the number of sub-committees and their conjoining staffs along with his commitment to rules making it more difficult to raise taxes and easier to cut spending. However, a rule change that would bar taxpayer money for special inter-est groups was a direct attack on the CBC. In the name of morality and fairness, stopping taxpayer money to special interest groups appears to bring neutrality and objectivity to legislative behavior and activity. In actuality, it cut a vital source of revenue to ethnic caucuses (Wines, 1994).

These changes altered how the CBC conducted the Annual Legislative Weekend. Due to this rule change, they could no longer have access to meeting rooms in the Capitol and would require much larger sponsor-ship packages for donors. This change also resulted in the increase in conference fees and the event to be solely run by the Congressional Black Caucus Foundation. Throughout the years, the foundation has evolved using different strategies in their mission, "to advance the global Black community by developing leaders, informing policy, and educat-ing the public" (CBC Foundation). Yet, the foundation has continued to help the Caucus:

> Facilitate the exchange of ideas and information to address critical issues affecting our communities. Promoting public health and financial empow-erment for all communities through innovative programs. Developing strategic research and historical resources for the public, academics, edu-cators, and students. All while providing leadership development and scholarship opportunities to educate the next generation of leaders.

Although evolution and growth among the Caucus have required a repo-sitioning, a fundamental understanding of the racialized structure, which persist in the U.S. Congress, is not lost among its membership. A recent example of the pervasiveness of the racialized structure in Congress is the thwarted congressional career of former Congresswoman Mia Love. Love of Utah's 4th district served in the 114th and 115th Congress as a member of the Republican Party. Her political career began as a city councilwoman for the city of Saratoga Springs, Utah, in 2003, where she made history as the first Haitian American elected official in Utah county (U.S. House of Representatives History, Art & Archives). She went on to become mayor of Saratoga Springs after serving on the council for 6 years and became a national star when speaking at the 2012 Republican National Convention. In this address, she leaned on her immigrant story of Haitian parents who fled the island nation due to political repression. Her story aligned with the idea that hard work and determination were the necessary ingredients for Black success in America. However, after winning the 4th congressional district in Utah, joining other legislators in Washington, she was no longer insulated as a conservative token and had to face her Blackness head on.

When Love arrived in DC for the 114th Congress, the political rhetoric of being in a post-racial era was all but gone. The Republican Party had been cuckolded by the Tea Party Caucus, which formed primarily out of their hatred of President Barack Obama, and his legislative success in the 111th Congress. During her campaign for the 4th congressional seat in Utah, she announced her intentions to join the CBC, in an effort to dismantle the caucus "from the inside out" (Henderson, 2015). The Republican Party had sold Congresswoman Love on her being the exception, with her invitation to speak at the 2012 National Convention. The myth of exceptionalism convinced her that she would not face the same plight as other Black legislators in Washington. Thus, she joined the CBC under the leadership of Congressman G. K. Butterfield, a centrist Democrat who like Love believed in a market-based approach to policy making. Upon joining the Caucus, she quickly learned that many of the assumptions that she had about the CBC were false. The procedural structure of the Caucus, which mimics the larger congressional procedural structure, made it difficult for a single representative to dismember the racial caucus, which had been established for 44 years.

Love's involvement in the Caucus proved to debunk the narrative of the Caucus instilling fear and blame by humanizing the members and exposing the cohesion that could exist across the aisle. That cohesion was seen in her advocation for immigration-related bills. The CBC had an extensive history in advocation for the Haitian people. On February 2, 1982, Congressman Dymally penned a letter asking Chairman Walter Fauntroy to name himself and Congresswoman Shirley Chisholm, both of

Caribbean heritage, to a special committee. The special committee could be comprised of whomever the chair selected but would be tasked with investigating the Haitian crisis. This special committee became the Haiti task force of present day.

The exceptionalism troupe that carried Congresswoman Love into office crumbled when President Donald Trump made vulgar and disparaging comments about immigrants, specifically ones from Haiti and other "Sh*thole countries" (Fram & Lemire, 2018). This presented Love with a moral dilemma; does she side with the new regime of her party, or does she stand up for the nation of her parents and ancestors? As a cosponsor of the Recognizing America's Children Act, her posture was clear, as the legislation allows for DACA recipients to remain in America. Love passed the chief moralist test, which was an indirect requirement for admission into the CBC yet was in opposition to her party's desire to promote White Supremacy in blackface.

Love's decision to defend her precious ancestral heritage ultimately cost her Utah's 4th district seat in Congress and presented her with the sobering reality of the racialized structure in Congress, exacerbated by the Republican Party. Had Love not ascribed to the tokenism presented to her by the Republican Party, the limited camaraderie found in her membership inside of the CBC may have extended her congressional career.

Scholarly literature categorizes representatives in an attempt to assess the effectiveness of representation especially in Congress. Descriptive representation is concerned often with the phenotypical or chosen identity of a representative in an effort to derive resemblance of those being represented. Symbolic representatives "stand for" and represent something meaningful for those being represented, whereas substantive representatives take actions on behalf of, in the interest of, as an agent of, and as a substitute for those being represented. The representatives that historically formed and continue to align with the CBC are most definitely descriptive representatives. This is punctuated by African American members in the 116th Congress that are not members of the CBC like Byron Donalds of Florida's 19th district, or Wesley Hunt of Texas' 38th district, or Senator Tim Scott a Senator from South Carolina. The melanin in one's skin does not immediately translate into an understanding of the political, economic, and social implications for what it means to be

Black in America. There are many African Americans who are insulated from discriminatory practices, which result in the inability to descriptively represent the interest of Black people, due to their insulation and disbelief in the need for pro-remedial policies (Lewis & Nelson, 2021).

The work of the CBC has long contested that they are descriptive, symbolic, and substantive representatives as they represent Black's access to full citizenship in the United States; the CBC members serve as a clarion call when the morality of legislation is under question. They are the agents for people who cannot speak for themselves. This is best exemplified in a statement made by Maxine Waters, a representative from California's 43rd district:

> ...even though the public does not know what you have prevented you know it is your responsibility whether people know what you are doing or even care about what you are doing you know it's your responsibility to avoid the constituents and the consumers of this country from getting ripped off, from being undermined, from being taken advantage of... (*Who I Am*, 2019)

Black Caucus members understand that they are called to occupy all three categories of representation. This was clear at their founding and remains clear among the members today. It is with that understanding and common belief that the CBC still votes as a left-wing bloc.

Black interests across the United States are divergent, and intersections of class, gender, religion, and education have become much more complex than at the CBC's founding (Devine, 1998). Yet, the CBC has never been a monolithic group and has always had a range of the ideological spectrum of integrationist and nationalist. This is seen historically in a letter penned to Congressman Ronald Dellums of California's 8th district from Michael Espy of Mississippi's 2nd district. Espy was asking for political cover as he was being "crucified" in the media for his neutrality in the Delta Pride Catfish plant workers strike in Indianola, MS. Espy justified his neutrality as a necessary measure for the brokering of a deal between the company's CEO Larry Joiner and the workers. Dellums, the Chairman of the CBC at the time known to be ideologically closer to Black Nationalism, believed Espy a pawn for White interest and responded in a letter dated October 7, 1990 (Ronald V. Dellums, Congressional Papers, 1990).

The divergence among the CBC was seen again with the Violent Crime Control and Law Enforcement Act of 1994, best known simply as the Crime Bill. The Violent Crime Control and Law Enforcement Act was a lengthy crime control bill that was put together over the course of 6 years. Its provisions implemented many things, including a "three strikes" mandatory life sentence for repeat offenders, money to hire 100,000 new police officers, $9.7 billion in funding for prisons, and an expansion of death penalty–eligible offenses. It also dedicated $6.1 billion to prevention programs.

To provide context, the "Crime Bill" was passed after the crack epidemic during the Reagan Administration. In many ways, legislation was poised to help localities deal with the challenges that cities were facing due to the infiltration of cocaine cooked to become crack. What was most inflammatory about the bill was its use of de facto segregation to disproportionately hurt Black communities. The bill allowed for steeper sentencing for the possession of crack cocaine instead of powdered cocaine, indirectly allowing longer sentences for Blacks who were more likely to be in possession of crack cocaine. There was no voting cohesion among CBC members. Ronald Dellums of California's 7th district, Maxine Waters of California's 35th district, and John Lewis of Georgia's 6th district all voted no. While Eddie Bernice Johnson of Texas' 30th district, Rep. Edolphus "Ed" Towns of New York's 10th district, and Bobby Rush of Illinois's 1st district voted yes.

Although the interest of Blacks in metropolitan cities may differ from rural Black interest and Blacks are not monolithic, they fundamentally agree that full citizenship is tied to having access to political power. Gaining access to that power through polity has been a war not yet won but progress achieved through the winning of battles in successive generations of the CBC. Black politics should be thought of as an extension of the universal power struggle, modified only by the condition that Whites occupy superordinate positions vis-à-vis Blacks, that this position is based on the institutionalized belief in the superiority of Whites, and that Whites act in a manner that will preserve their superordinate position (M. Jones, 2014). The perseveration of this power and position is through legislation that often seeks to codify White superiority.

The founding of the CBC and its continued existence is the signal of Black willingness to fight and secure power in an effort to dismantle the White superordinate position. Many decry the power secured by the CBC is cuckolded by a Washington legislative process and that its growth from 13 members to a historic 60 in the 116th Congress is no more than symbolism. Yet, a historic review in concert with the resistance seen inside of Congress tells a different story. The legislative structure by nature is systematically restrained, yet the CBC has still found a way to be the voice of the voiceless. The legislative success rate averages 3%. However, the 111th Congress, when the CBC had decentralized power through committee saturation, was the most productive congressional session since the 89th Congress in 1965 to 1967 before the Caucus was founded. Such productivity can be attributed to the Democratic Party having the majority in the House, the Senate, and occupancy in the White House. Yet, the Democratic Party leadership was filled with CBC members, which included the first Black man to become the president of the United States.

A review of the historical archives don't show a commitment to producing a Black president, but it surely shows a commitment to a policy agenda that is concerned with the least of these. Historically, Blacks in the United States have been among the least of these. The lack of access to polity has contributed to Blacks remaining the least of these, which is why the Black Declaration of Independence that came from the National Black Political Conference is an important foundation for how the CBC developed a policy platform (Black Declaration of Independence, n.d.).

The notoriety of CBC members at the founding came through the use of floor speeches, interviews with the press, and meetings with the president to implore him to use his bully-pulpit for issues they deemed paramount. Congressional scholars describe these actions as legislative behavior; the acumen and strategy needed to be a successful legislator (Meller, 1960). The CBC has seen legislative success in social welfare, labor, education, healthcare, and civil rights.

Housing insecurity continues to be a major political interest of Blacks. The National Alliance to End Homelessness reports that African Americans and Indigenous people experience homelessness at higher rates than Whites (Homelessness and Racial Disparities, 2025). These debilitating circumstances most definitely encroaches upon one's ability to pursue happiness. Without reliable housing, it is difficult to participate as a full citizen of the United States. This handicap is experienced by Blacks largely due to long-standing historical and structural racism. The housing phenomenon of redlining seen through the use of governmental programs in the north is complimented by the land acquisition by governmental entities in the south.

This is why the appointment and tenure of Marcia Fudge to the Department of Housing and Urban Development, a former CBC member representing the state of Ohio, are important. Secretary Fudge was the first Black woman to hold the position in 40 years (Jan, 2021). She was the former Chairwoman of the CBC and served in the 113th Congressional session. Her previous committee assignment on the House Education and Labor Committee helped her understand the relevant issues that lead to being insecure. Secretary Fudge is also clear about how governmental programs have been used to systematically perpetuate racist stereotypes that plague American minority populations especially Black communities. The CBC's consistent commitment to the social welfare of Blacks has been noticeable over the last 50 years. Republican as well as Democratic Presidential Administrations have become accustomed to the organized strategies used by the members of the CBC. Yet, neither party was prepared for the execution of these practices to land one of their very own in a presidential cabinet post as the chief executioner of housing policies.

Blacks, who are among the lowest earners, need to get a college education that will greatly guarantee students' financial stability. Such stability will help with raising Blacks out of the lowest income rungs. In the quest to attain that bachelor's degree, Blacks have relied on HBCUs. HBCUs make up only 3% of the country's colleges and universities, but enroll 10% of all Black students and produce almost 20% of all Black graduates (Bridges, 2020).

Therefore, H.R. 5363: the FUTURE Act of 2019 signed in the 116th Congress most assuredly aligns with Blacks and their interest. The bill was sponsored by Alma Adams of North Carolina's 12th district, the home of Johnson C. Smith University, a HBCU founded in 1867, aligned with the Presbyterian Church. FUTURE is the acronym for Fostering Undergraduate Talent by Unlocking Resources for Education:

This bill permanently authorizes funding for minority-serving institutions of higher education and increases the authorization of appropriations for Pell Grants. This bill directs the Internal Revenue Service (IRS), upon the written request of the Department of Education (ED), to disclose to any authorized person, tax return information to determine eligibility for recertification for income-contingent or income-based repayments of student loans, discharges of loans based on total and permanent disability, and the amount of student financial aid under the Higher Education Act of 1965. The IRS must also establish and implement procedures for re-certifying income for purposes of this bill and for requesting tax return information. The bill requires ED and the IRS to issue joint reports to Congress on this bill, including an update on the status of implementation of this bill and an evaluation of how such implementation affected the processing of applications for financial aid and discharge of student loans (H.R. 5363).

The permanent authorization used in this bill uses the budget authority from the Higher Education Act of 1965, which is why this bill was not referred to a committee, instead it was voted on the House Floor as a roll-call vote. Many may see this legislation as an automatic and might miss the skill of Congresswoman Adams. She was keen to place a provision in the act that allowed for an increase in Pell Grants. These grants are offered to low-income students who the IRS decides are not required to contribute to their collegiate education. Congresswoman Adams was also savvy enough to include a report that must be submitted to the House Education and Workforce Committee of which she is a member.

The bill ensures fiscal normalcy for HBCUs. Many of those institutions rely on the Title III funds allocated in the Higher Education Act of 1965 released with the FUTURE Act. With Blacks being among the lowest earners in the United States, this bill helps with securing funding through the expansion of Pell Grants; protects income-based repayment programs for students who have student loan debt; and builds in an oversight requirement with a joint report that informs Congress of the success of discharged student loans. Such a report was politically savvy as Betsy DeVos' Department of Education inside of the 1st Trump Administration was proven slow and arguably negligent in the discharge of student loan debt for those enrolled in income-based or special provision repayment plans (Green & Cowley, 2019). Research shows that Blacks are more likely to default on their student loans:

> Black or African American borrowers remain higher than those of their peers, regardless of the type of higher education institution they attended. Within six years of starting college, one-third of all Black or African American borrowers who had entered repayment defaulted on their loans, compared to just 13 percent of their white peers. (Miller, 2019)

Therefore, programs assisting in accumulating less student loan debt and helping with repayment will most definitely help Blacks.

On December 19, 2019, a deadly virus emerged in China and spread person to person through droplets released into the air when an infected person coughs or sneezes. The symptoms mimic those of the flu and in severe cases can lead to respiratory problems, kidney failure, and death (Sauer, 2020). The pandemic disproportionally hurt Blacks throughout the country, and CBC members pushed the conversation about these disparities through the introduction of legislation, press conferences, and virtual town hall meetings with their constituents. At the surge of the global pandemic in March 2020, CBC members Congresswoman Barbara Lee, and then Chairwoman Karen Bass bombarded the news cycle advocating for the Trump presidential administration to release data that would show the infection, and survival rate of the virus by ethnicity and race (Lee, 2020). Both women have a history of being intimately concerned with the health disparities of Blacks throughout the country and suspected what we later learned to be true. Black people were almost three times more likely to die of the virus than their White counterparts (Ray, 2020). Congresswoman Barbara Lee, a CBC member and former chairwoman, was among the lawmakers that introduced H.R. 6585 the Equitable Data Collection and Disclosure on COVID-19 Act on April 14, 2020:

> The legislation comes as reports across the United States point to stark racial disparities in COVID-19 cases and fatalities. In Michigan, Black residents account for 33% of confirmed COVID-19 cases and 40% of fatalities, despite making up only 14% of the state's population. In Louisiana, 70% of those who have died from COVID-19 so far are Black,

compared with 32% of the state's population. Initial data from Boston shows that among people whose race was reported, more than 40 percent of people infected with COVID-19 were Black, despite making up just 25% of the city's population. (Barbra Lee's Office, 2020)

These data were made available due to the pressure produced by the CBC. Such disparities are signs of institutional and systematic racism as Blacks disproportionately suffer from the preexisting conditions that make the virus more lethal. Underlying health conditions such as high blood pressure, diabetes, obesity, chronic lung disease, and kidney disease are prevalent in Black communities (Howard, 2020). These health disparities are linked to geography where Blacks have faced redlining (Jan, 2018), which has led to food insecurity exasperating health conditions. Years of committee and subcommittee work alongside Caucus task forces allowed the Caucus and its members to be clear about the systematic health disparities. This understanding was built on decades of work that resulted in national attention for Black communities during the pandemic.

Names like Mia Love of Utah's 4th district or Marcia Fudge of Ohio's 11th district are foreign to average Black Americans; yet, their impact on the advocacy of Black interest across the ideological spectrum cannot be denied. Fudge, the Chairwoman for the CBC in the 113th Congress during the presidency of Barack Obama, helped to reshape the housing industry after the subprime mortgage crisis of 2007, which lasted until 2010, and Mia Love decided to take the moral high ground during the Trump administration as a member of the Republican Party. Yet, Love is largely invisible, unlike Liz Cheney who made a similar decision as the cochair of the January 6th Commission. Although Fudge and Love are women at the opposite ends of the ideological spectrum, neither of them are widely recognized for their contributions in protecting the interest of Black Americans. This is in part caused by the belief that Black women are not seen as rational actors.

Rationality, which is decided upon by an individual's choices, requires anticipation of the outcomes. Theoretically, rational actors review the options before them alongside the known alternative courses of action. The calculation of the best strategy establishes rational actors (Goldthorpe, 1998). However, the idea of the best strategy is subjective as it does not inherently consider societal restraints. Those restraints affect the selection of a strategy and the use of resources available to a rational actor. Their known resources often align with the following categories: time, information, approval, and prestige. It is with these resources that rational actors develop alternative choices and strategies that produce optimal outcomes.

Men are societally viewed as rational actors because they choose alternatives that often lead to their greatest satisfaction. This in turn creates a social order, which champions strategies that lead to individual satisfaction instead of collective stability. A rational actor is defined as a conscious social actor engaging in deliberate calculative strategies (Goldthorpe, 1998). Yet, there is a particular set or system of linked social structures that are needed for relating and behaving. These linked social structures often make it difficult for women, particularly Black women, to be seen as rational actors.

Kimberly Crenshaw in 1991 uses the law to reveal the intersecting oppressions Black women experience due to the American societal structure. The concept of Intersecting Oppressions recognizes that African American women's distinct obstacles are a result of the convergence of their racial and gender identities. Intersectionality seeks to understand the interaction between various social identities and how these interactions define societal power hierarchies (Else-Quest & Hyde, 2016; Shames, 2017; Wright-Austin & Ford, 2023). The use of intersectionality with an examination of the unique effects of systemic hurdles, prejudices, and biases on Black women helps to examine their lack of perceived rationality. Black women's lack of access to rational resources is often determined by the societal power hierarchies discussed in Crenshaw's work. Such systems of power leave the rational resources of approval and prestige outside of the grasp of Black women often making them visible and invisible simultaneously.

African American women's voices have been historically and systematically excluded from scholarly literature (Muhs, 2012). The awareness of intersectionality in this work can best acknowledge why the behaviors and choices of Black women are excluded. Often, Black women focus on the driving force of political action wrought with racism, sexism, or homophobia. This focus makes them visible as drivers of change to societal power hierarchies, which often categorize them as less than. Such a choice in focus is seen to be in abstention to assumed norms rendering them invisible to the larger society.

A Black woman's decision to inject their lived experiences, and the experiences of others directly affected by the policy decisions of others, is a strategy used to increase visibility. Without visibility, a Black woman's choice is deemed trite and incapable of approval. This exclusively removes Black women's access to the rational resources of prestige and approval. Yet, Black women as legislators must still engage in congressional norms despite their diminutive status. The racial hierarchy established alongside the gender hierarchy in this country, and subsequently in political science, has shaped its societal norms. It has also simultaneously made it impossible for Black women to interact with morality, cooperation, and trust the way a White male can. Simply, approval and subsequent prestige is only ascribed to chief executive decision makers who are often White males. This assertion is supported in the U.S. Congress where ethnic diversity has increased, but the body still does not reflect the growing ethnic population.

White Americans make up a larger share of Congress than they do in the U.S. population at 75% of Congress and only 59% of the population (Schaeffer, 2023). This is exacerbated by the number of White males in Congress who make up 50% of the 535-member body. Access to the full cadre of rational resources, which include time, information, approval, and prestige, is reserved for White men as a preservation of societal power hierarches discussed by Crenshaw. Therefore, the presence of a Black woman in Congress places stress on these structures and challenges the society to rethink the lens in which power is exercised. Such reevaluation requires scholarship to examine the lack of access to rationality for Black women legislators that render them invisible.

The proceeding chapters in the book seek to take the women of the CBC from invisible to visible. Such visibility is in apart due to the expansion in scholarly literature about Black women. Pearl Dowe engaged the foundational political science theory of political ambition. Her examination resulted in the expansion of the theory to include an understanding of how Black women navigate political choices, opportunities, and obstacles. The theoretical expansion included the strategy of leveraging Black organizations and networks for voter mobilization, fundraising, and overall success while in office(Dowe, 2020).

Understanding the political behavior of the women of the CBC is acknowledging the well-known, as well as the not-so-well-known, women of this Caucus in its over 50-year history. Dowe's work lays the groundwork for the idea that Black women have indeed been rational actors with their use of strategies particularly suited for Black women due to intersecting oppression. A review of the role of unknown names in successive chapters will establish a pattern supported by the strategies Dowe presents in her work. An historic evaluation of the women of the CBC will illuminate invisible work done by Black women for successive generations, and how it can help in identifying the next generation of Black female congressional leaders in an effort to make them visible.

# CHAPTER 2

## The Foundational Women of the Congressional Black Caucus

The CBC was founded during an era of American history that saw an expansion in rights. In 1958, in the District of Columbia two residents of Virginia, Mildred Jeter, a Black woman, and Richard Loving, a White man, were married. Obtaining a marriage license in the nation's capital violated the anti-miscegenation statute in Virginia that banned interracial marriages. Virginia, once the headquarters of the confederacy, charged the couple with violating the state law shortly after the Lovings returned to Virginia. The Lovings were found guilty and they were sentenced to a year in jail, which lead to successive appeal that ultimately landed the case in the Supreme Court. In April 1967, close to a decade after their marriage, the Constitution question remained: Did Virginia's anti-miscegenation law violate the Equal Protection Clause of the Fourteenth Amendment? In June 1967, a unanimous decision, by the Court deemed Virginia's anti-miscegenation law did violate the Equal Protection Clause effectively allowing interracial marriage.

The Supreme Court's decision is historically known for the ending of a ban on interracial marriage. However, a historical review of the case denotes the genesis of the second wave of feminism that expanded women's rights. In 1970, Jane Roe filed a lawsuit against Henry Wade, the district attorney of Dallas County, TX, challenging a law that made abortion illegal except by a doctor's orders to save a woman's life. There were multiple constitutional conflicts wrapped up in the First, Fourth, Fifth, Ninth, and Fourteenth Amendments. Yet, the constitutional question was clear: Does the Constitution recognize a woman's right to terminate her pregnancy by abortion? In January 1973, the Court decided the Texas law violated the Fourteenth Amendment effectively granting a woman the right to terminate a pregnancy.

Unlike the Loving case *Roe v. Wade* was not unanimous leaving two justices who dissented. They believed the fetus had access to the same rights afforded the mother pursuant to the Fourteenth Amendment. It is quite ironic that the constitutional amendment created to ensure African American citizenship after the Civil War is the same amendment responsible for expanding the rights of all women. Such expansion is coupled with successive Civil Rights Acts of 1957, 1960, 1964, and 1965. The expansion of rights for women simultaneously with the expansion of the rights of Blacks undoubtedly acted as a precursor for the formation of the CBC and the first generation of Black women who would lead this budding caucus.

Black women, as a group, were made visible in the Loving case because of the unanimous ruling in favor of a Black woman's choice to marry a White man; yet this visibility is undermined because the court was ruling far more on the rationality of a White man's right of choice in marriage than hers. The supposed victory for equity seen in *Roe v. Wade* is fleeting because the court was not ruling on Black women's right to choose in motherhood but primarily focused on White women, another group who is not required to compete with intersecting oppressions.

The decisions in *Loving v Virginia* and *Roe v. Wade* inadvertently dealt with the socialization and formation of families. Loving expanded the eligible pool of people that any person could marry and *Roe v. Wade* allowed all women the right to determine whether they would have children and how many. Neither of these Supreme Court rulings had intention on advancing the political or social standing of Black women, but Black women used these rulings to empower themselves and actualize their political ambition. Political ambition has been studied extensively and Joseph Schlesinger, the foundational scholar of political ambition theory, focuses on the political consequences of ambition honing in on those who hold office. Schlesinger (1966) drives the idea of individual motivation and the need for sufficient resources. He argues that the effective use of resources and clear strategies win political campaigns. Yet, Black women's ambition for running is not rooted in personal ambition.

Dowe, in "Resisting marginalization: Black women's political ambition and agency," widens the lens through which Black women are viewed and their political agency can be assessed. Dowe argues that when we think about the political ambition of women we are inherently concentrating on White women, negating the existence of Black women on the political landscape (Dowe, 2020). This narrow scope limits our understanding of political ambition and doesn't provide room for the true political ambitions of Black women, which is often the collective. To best understand, Dowe expands the framework to include the political tenants of choices, opportunities, and obstacles. This emphasis is important for understanding the political behavior of Black women as their ambitions are driven by collectivity not by individualism, which doesn't fit political norms.

Dowe in *Radical Imagination of Black Women* (2024) argues that elite Black women have a unique political ambition that compels them to move beyond service to seek office. She supports the idea that Black women's unique experience of being Black and woman requires a grappling with their intersecting oppression, thus shaping their worldview. This view directly affects how they address and understand their position within society, and their subsequent commitment to their community. Dowe correctly identified these women as mostly college-educated, middle-class super joiners: members of multiple civic, religious, and political organizations whose active membership in these groups undergird their ambition and eventual pursuit of political position. This leadership pursuit is complicated by the equal compulsion to cause the most covert ripple to the political stream.

These women utilized the social networks of sororities, institutional resources of the Black Church and HBCUs, and their ability to activate the communities they desire to politically represent, to both be voted to political office and advance the cause of their constituents. This is simultaneously done without really threatening the established top executive office within their individual states or being seen as a viable candidate for the President of the United States as Shirley Chisolm tested out in 1972. One of the factors may be that if they sought to be elected governor of a state, it would overextend their political currency and may prove to exhaust their political capital. This would destroy the potential of returning to their communities in an effort to mobilize the people who they have just disappointed with their losing effort.

This first wave of female CBC members possessed a moral obligation and tether to their community and its advancement because women are the natural culture carriers within the Black family. Each one of these women has a seemingly unbreakable tie to their community and the people who make up their constituency. Black women who actualize their political ambition, even if that ambition is motivated primarily by seeking power, cannot untie themselves from the communities that sent them to the legislature. This is a direct result of the fact that virtually all the organizations they are a member of have concern for the collective at their core.

For Black women, the collective is empowering because it provides a direct benefactor of the choices, opportunities, and obstacles uniquely presented by their intersecting oppressions. The collective helps Black women cultivate self-efficacy, assurance, and the capacity to exert influence over people in surrounding environments. As culture carriers, Black women are often instigating transformation in their environments, which requires mobilization and collaboration. The ability to collaborate and sufficiently mobilize is possible through empowerment. Empowerment theory is based on the idea that human problems are a result of a social, political, and economic environment that is oppressive to those with fewer advantages. The theory also recognizes that individuals and communities are interdependent and mutually influence each other.

However, empowerment theory does not extend the influence of those seen in disadvantaged communities as leaders to the highest political offices in the land. This is seen clearly in the legislative insignificance of the foundational female CBC members. Such insignificance explains these women choose not to pursue seats in the U.S. Senate because this would be seen as "asking for too much too soon" or "outlandish."

Yet, Black women's strategic, deliberate, and constant political engagement does gain them some political influence (Dowe, 2024). In the case of the foundational women of the CBC, it gets them elected to Congress after serving in their respective state legislatures. This is in large part due to their radical imaginations, which first asserts that Black women's strategic, deliberate, and constant political engagement will produce results. The result is attached to their conscious decision making about the offices they chose to seek, doing an assessment of which office enables the greatest community impact, and an assessment on how to best navigate a marginalizing political structure. The marginalization still requires these Black female legislatures to operate in some degree of obscurity. The intersecting oppressions of sexism and racism, which are so overtly prevalent within the United States, often limit the resources or the support Black women need in seeking political office.

Congresswomen within the CBC have to manage their visibility in their communities while contending with invisibility in the larger legislature. The invisibility they encounter is rooted in the assumption that they are irrational actors, which is the opposite of the assumption of the rationality ascribed to the White men in the legislature. Black women in politics are concerned with their continued visibility to the Black community and respective communities, because such visibility was established by becoming fixtures within that community. The lack of universal access to the political structure in the Black community often wins Black women the moniker of "advocate who gets things done for us."

Nevertheless, Black Congresswomen must still contend with their invisibility in the larger legislature. Two of the rational resources approval and prestige are often unavailable to Black female legislatures because of the causes they support. Chisholm, along with Barbara Jordan, Yvonne Burke, and Cardiss Collins are the foundational pillars who do the invisible work of establishing the CBC we know today. Upon the shoulders of these ladies, future generations of female CBC members have built their political standing. These groundbreaking women used the political ambition as described by Dowe in *The Radical Imagination of Black Women* to leverage the Supreme Court decisions discussed earlier. The election of these women from 1969 to 1982 sought to normalize their presence inside of the political landscape and maximize on the implications of the previously discussed court cases. All these pillars, minus Collins, who won a special election following her husband's death, served in their state legislature prior to being elected to Congress. These women may not have gained the approval of those in the larger political landscape, yet their service in their respective states lead to their election to the U.S. House of Representatives (Table 2.1).

**Table 2.1** Congressional Black Caucus Female Pillars

| Female Pillar | State and Congressional District | Congressional Terms and Years Served | Total Number of Bills Sponsored | Total Number of Bills Cosponsored |
|---|---|---|---|---|
| Shirley Chisholm | New York's 10th district | 91st–97th (1968–1982) | 64 | 1,783 |
| Yvonne Brathwaite Burke | California's 37th district 28th district | 93rd (1973–1975) 94th–95th (1975–1979) | 97 | 817 |
| Cardiss Collins | Illinois, 7th district | 93rd–104th (1973–1997) | 466 | 4,918 |
| Barbara C. Jordan | Texas, 18th district | 93rd–95th (1973–1979) | 40 | 267 |

Shirley Chisholm is well respected as the first Black woman to serve in the U.S. House of Representatives, yet was largely invisible in the larger political landscape. Her conscious decision about the office to seek was guided by district realignment in 1966. Chisolm's assessment of greatest community impact through office held acknowledges the inclusion of majority Black neighborhoods Bedford-Stuyvesant and Central Brooklyn into the 12th district. Such assessment had her to leave the state legislature becoming the representative of New York's 12th district from 1968 to 1982 in the 91st–97th Congresses.

Before her election to Congress, she worked as a teacher and school director in New York. As a child of Jamaican immigrants, she understood education to be the great equalizer and her commitment to education was seen while she served on the Education Committee in the House. One-sixth of the legislation she sponsored was related to education with a deliberate focus on Black colleges and compulsory education. H.R. 5680 (96th): Higher Education Amendments of 1980 sought to:

> amend the Higher Education Act of 1965 to strengthen and improve the student loan programs so as to assure the availability of funds to students to attend the institution of higher education of their choice, to strengthen the procedures for the repayment of such loans, and for other purposes.

The legislation did not make it out of committee; this is of note because Chisholm sat on said committee. Although a visible advocate in her community and notable member of the CBC as its very first woman, her sponsorship of a bill that would fundamentally change the method in which higher education was financed was outside the reach of a Black woman.

During Shirley Chisholm's tenure, she sponsored 31 bills in total with only one signed and enacted into law. Although legislative success can be contributed to many variables, a review of the legislation sponsored by Chisholm exposes strong liberal views that were focused on the collective. With such strong views, Chisholm's assessment on how to best navigate the marginalizing political structure in the House of Representatives meant sponsorship of House Resolutions. Resolutions are not laws; rather, they are expressions of the "sentiments" of either the House or Senate. Therefore, Chisholm combated invisibility inside of the larger political structure with symbolic acts that would keep her visibly working for those who are forgotten and dismissed.

As previously discussed, the members of the CBC are descriptive and symbolic representatives charged with bringing back substantive legislation to their communities. In the foundational years of this racial Caucus, the art of being a good legislator was constantly being developed. These foundational women understood the political structure was designed to marginalize them at best and ignore them at worst; therefore, each of them did not become fixated on the passing of legislation but instead was committed to providing the greatest impact.

Dowe describes elite Black women who seek office as women who assess the political landscape. The accumulation of power is not at the forefront of their decision to run and does not become their goal once in the selected office. Shirley Chisholm definitely fit the description because during her tenure, she sponsored 33 House Resolutions and 27 of them were agreed upon as simple resolutions. Her understanding of marginalization in a political structure and astute understanding of the lawmaking process, fed from her NY State Assembly experience, gave her a proven strategy for greatest impact. A review of three of her House Resolutions, which were agreed upon as simple resolutions, demonstrates her commitment to the community and the collective.

H.R. 272 (96th): A resolution providing for the consideration of the bill (H.R. 2641) to amend section 106 of the Civil Rights Act of 1957 to raise the limitation on appropriations for the U.S. Commission on Civil Rights. This piece of legislation is critically important in providing the necessary funding to a commission established to investigate the violation of civil rights primarily by southern states. The Civil Rights Act of 1957 is the foundational Civil Rights Act, which is followed by an Act in 1960, 1964 and in 1965. Sections 4 and 5 of the Civil Rights Act of 1965 required states with a history of discrimination to check with the commission before making changes. Funding for this commission was imperative to protect the rights of Blacks; Chisholm's legislative existence in the House is tangential to the Civil Rights Act of 1965 passed 3 years before her election to the House. This resolution does not directly affect her constituents in New York's 12th district, but it supports Chisholm's commitment to Black people once in office.

H.R. 569 (95th): A resolution providing for the consideration of H. R. 1139, a bill to extend through fiscal year 1982 certain child nutrition programs under the National School Lunch Act and the Child Nutrition Act of 1966. The National School Lunch Act and the Child Nutrition Act of 1966 established the school breakfast program that we know today, providing nutritionally balanced, low-cost or free breakfast to children primarily in public schools. Chisholm's commitment to advocating on behalf of those whom she represented was steadfast; she knows that with the advent of Reaganomics, an already vulnerable segment of society, the poor and very poor children, would be in danger of losing a valuable resource. This directly impacts Chisholm's 12th district based on the number of children who would be taking advantage of this program.

H.R. 1208 (95th): A resolution providing for the consideration of H.R. 15, a bill to extend for 5 years certain elementary, secondary, and other education programs. Chisholm offers this resolution in a savvy exercise of leveraging the lawmaking process and committee appointment to help marginalized communities who needed these programs. Chisholm, who was on the education committee, takes it upon herself to bring attention to a piece of legislation that by May 1978 had stalled in committee since January of the previous year. Her acumen and adroit legislative skill are on display by bringing a finite 5-year extension to the fund, which coerces the members into a roll-call vote. Chisholm's resolution allows the legislation to reach the House Floor bypassing the consternation of the committee, while providing a term limit for the law ensuring easier passage by roll-call vote on the House Floor. These funds would be to help children in low-income areas who are educationally deprived or have special needs, while bolstering Title I schools and their subsequent programs. In addition, school districts would be able to use enrollment data rather than area residency to be eligible for these funds, making it accessible to children in unstable living situations. This legislation was significant in Chisholm being continually seen as a dedicated advocate for those in her district.

Shirley Chisholm's radical imagination mixed well with the more liberal, anti-Vietnam War environment that was housed inside of her district; this made getting elected to Congress feasible in New York. Her time in the state assembly had established a track record of advocacy for marginalized communities and the issues that directly affected them. She was not seen as a participant in maintaining the status quo and her famous motto of "Unbought and Unbossed" stuck with her constituents and resonated with people in other parts of the nation as well. Her radical imagination also coinciding with the Women's liberation movement of the late 1960s and early 1970s, yet intersecting oppressions and the struggle for visibility in the larger legislative structure remained, even within the CBC.

Yvonne Brathwaite Burke was the representative of California's 28th Congressional District from 1973 to 1979 (93rd–95th Congresses), and her short but impactful tenure in Congress was filled with firsts. She, before she arrived in DC, had already been the first Black woman to be elected as a representative within the California State Assembly. Burke arrived for the 93rd Congress as the first Black woman representative from the west coast of the country. In addition, she was the first member of Congress to have given birth during her term as well as the first female member of Congress to be granted maternity leave after the birth of her daughter, Autumn.

Burke is also of great note because she was the first female head of the CBC. She was extremely visible within the Black communities that she represented yet still battled invisibility in the larger legislative body. This is evidenced by only two of her 92 pieces of legislation being enacted into law during her tenure. The severe disparity of legislation sponsored by these foundational CBC women enacted into law speaks directly to the uphill climb of being visible or seen in the larger legislative bodies.

Burke's legislative career, though brief, was intentional to advocate for issues that effected Black communities including equal opportunity initiatives for women and the poor. Burke used her appointment to the House Appropriations Committee to increase funding for federal desegregation mandates aimed at local jurisdictions across the nation. Burke also sponsored H.R. 10126 (95th Congress), which required heads of government agencies to establish and maintain a program for part-time career federal employees (mostly minorities) to be eligible for healthcare and other benefits on a prorated scale. Burke's political career could have been longer within Congress, but her choice to not seek reelection and run to be the Attorney General of California seems to coincide with a concern with motherhood, another area of invisibility that Black women have to encounter.

By 1978, when she departs Congress to go try and return to state politics, her daughter Autumn would have been starting grade school. Although she did not return to Congress, she was called upon by President Barack Obama to serve on the board of directors for Amtrak, and in 2014, upon Autumn's election to the California State Assembly, they became the first mother-and-daughter pair to have served in that legislative body. Congresswoman Burke's bid for Attorney General in California, while unsuccessful, sets the stage for another woman who would become the Attorney General of California in 2011 and later become a member of the CBC: Kamala Harris.

Cardiss Collins of Illinois' 7th Congressional district held office from 1973 to 1997 (93rd–104th Congresses). Collins' political career was foundational for Black female CBC members in a few significant ways. She was the first Black woman to represent the Midwestern portion of the country, and the first chairwomen of the CBC. Congresswoman Collins had the longest tenure of these foundational CBC women and was the only Black woman in the U.S. legislature for 6 years from the 99th to the 102nd Congress. She was also the only foundational CBC woman who did not serve in her state's legislature before coming to Congress. Her entry into Congress came as a result of her husband's death in December 1972 in a plane crash, just after he had been elected for a second term (Yardley, 2013). This speaks to her indirect knowledge of the legislative process via her husband's time in Congress, giving her the opportunity to see his errors and not duplicate them.

Collins got to actualize her radical imagination inside of getting legislation passed into law because of how the culture of America shifted during her tenure. Her congressional career spans a period of time in the nation where the series of Civil Rights Act(s) from the 1950s to 1960s, and Supreme Court decisions like *Loving v. Virginia* and *Roe v. Wade* were no longer seen as cutting edge. This allowed for the creation of institutions that sought to codify the rights gained through the judiciary and through legislation. Collins extended tenure in the House of Representatives, where she saw the effective use of institutions, encouraged her to join 14 other Black women forming the African-American Women for Reproductive Freedom. The organization was meant to expose the nuanced aspects of stigma and historic trauma associated with Black women and reproductive health in 1990 (#TRUST Black women, n.d.). This organization was the foundation for Black women's reproductive rights and can be credited for the plethora of organizations like Black Women's Reproductive Justice Organizations, Black Women for Wellness (CA), Black Women's Health Imperative (national), SisterLove (GA), and SPARK Reproductive Justice Now! (GA).

Collins was highly visible in the areas of gender equity in healthcare, college sports, and welfare issues. Such visibility was keenly used in her position as CBC chair when critical issues arose in the Presidency of Jimmy Carter, which was duplicated during the Clinton Administration even though she was not the CBC chairwoman. Her tenure and mindfulness allow for a diverse legislative portfolio, which includes child care programs and children's safety. Her invisibility inside of the larger political landscape results in the lack of attribution for meaningful societal shifts through the use of House Resolutions.

For 3 years, Collins sponsored House Resolutions designating October as breast cancer awareness month: H.J.Res. 570 in the 101st, H.J.Res. 38 in the 102nd, H.J.Res. 257 in the 102nd, and H.J.Res. 393 in the 102nd. Collins persistence resulted in President Bill Clinton signing H.J.Res. 11 in the 103rd permanently making October Breast Cancer Awareness Month. These efforts were after she advocated for a Working Mother Day in 1981. As an advocate for women and children, Collins sponsored

H.R. 965 Child Safety Protection Act in the 103rd without a cosponsor. The law ensured that small toys, which had been dangerous choking hazard for children, were mandated to be labeled as such on the packaging. This legislation also included children's bicycle safety measures, which encouraged the wearing of helmets and other safety equipment. Her steadfast commitment to produce legislation supported Black motherhood and overall health, and her tenure did not require permission from the larger legislative apparatus.

Congresswoman Collins is still largely invisible to the political imagination of the American public. This may be in fact because the legislation discussed above is seen as insignificant. However, this could not be further from the truth; the combination of notable pieces of legislation and her legislative effectiveness shows that even legislative success does not guarantee approval or prestige. Collins was able to get signed into law more legislation than any single member of the CBC of present (Nelson, 2022). Such an accomplishment solidified her as someone who got things done, which included being ranked #13 of 212 Democrats in the 104th Congress. Ironically, she is largely obscure and invisible even among the Black population that she once fought for. The inability of Black women to be seen as rational actors consistently finds them doing the work without proper attribution.

Congresswoman Katie B. Hall represented Indiana's 1st district in the U.S. House of Representatives from 1982 to 1985 (97th–98th Congresses), and Hall was the first African American representative from Indiana of any gender. Hall's political career, similar to most of the foundational CBC women, began in both the Indiana House of Representatives and state Senate before making her way to the U.S. Congress. One of the items that links Congresswomen Katie Hall and Cardiss Collins together is that a special election following death that opened up the door for them both. For Collins, it was her husband's sudden death in a plane crash and for Hall, it was the death of her predecessor, Adam Benjamin, Jr., that allowed her ascension.

The primary legislative achievement of Hall's tenure in Congress was being able to get Rev. Dr. Martin Luther King, Jr.'s, birthday made into a national holiday in 1983. This legislation had failed to be adopted for

14 years prior. Hall used H.R. 3706 in the 98th Congress to make the third Monday in January, a federal holiday to honor Dr. King's life. Hall's visibility in the process of getting this national holiday adopted is prominent; yet, her congressional career was probably cut short based on her push for this holiday.

The congressional tenure of Hall highlights the intersecting oppressions that Black women in politics must face consistently. Her district, which includes one of the largest Black populations in the state of Indiana, elects a White man rather than Hall in a three-person primary. Her defeat in the primary seems to forget that her voting record advocated for measures that would reduce substance abuse, bankruptcy, and unemployment within the district. This points again to the contrast that Black women have to wrestle with the fact that, being effective in getting legislation passed into law is not enough to make them visible, keep them in office, or gain them prestige. Hall was narrowly defeated in her reelection bid in 1984 by less than 2,400 votes and lost in two subsequent attempts to regain that same seat.

Texas Congresswoman Barbara C. Jordan is one of the most instrumental foundational CBC members in addition to representing the 18th Congressional District of Texas from 1973 to 1979 (93rd–95th Congresses). She was a trailblazer in significant ways and lays the groundwork for increased visibility among CBC women and advanced the fight against invisibility for the women behind her. Jordan's political career begins within the unlikely state legislature of Texas and then the state Senate, where she was the first Black woman to serve and first Black female President Pro Tempore in 1972. Ironically, she got a chance to serve as the acting governor of Texas for a day.

Her congressional district was the result of the Civil Rights Act of 1965 voting parameters and coupled with the 1970 U.S. Census; there was a new congressional seat that needed to be filled in a majority Black-populated area of Texas that included Houston.

For other foundational CBC women, motherhood and marriage were two spaces used to normalize their presence politically. Jordan's invisibility may have been fed by the fact that she was neither married nor a mother. These factors are in direct contrast to her fellow fresh women CBC peers of 1973, Yvonne Burke and Cardiss Collins. Burke was granted maternity leave during her first term, and Collins became a Congresswoman as a result of her spouse's death.

Although Jordan was quite visible on the national political landscape because of her oratorical skill and commonsense style of explanation, she is still overlooked when thinking about prominent members of Congress in the 20th century. Her speech during the Nixon impeachment hearings is ranked 13th among the 100 best American political speeches of the 20th century, and it televised her incredible rhetorical expertise that she had been honing for years (Lucas & Medhurst, 2009). Congresswoman Jordan had been crafting her masterful use of language as a nationally recognized debater at Texas Southern University, a historically Black university, taking on and defeating Ivy League competitors. She had also heard plenty of arguments being made from her father in the pulpit on Sunday mornings.

Congresswoman Jordan fits into Dowe's description of those prominent Black women who have been elected to public office. Jordan's upbringing as a preacher's daughter within the Black Church, along with graduating from an HBCU (Texas Southern University), joining a sorority (Delta Sigma Theta Sorority, Inc.) and participation in civic organizations (National Associate for the Advancement of Colored People [NAACP], National and Texas Democratic Conventions) gave credence to her radical imagination and political ambition that landed her in Congress as one of the foundational women within the CBC.

Congresswoman Jordan's visibility was critical in holding the country and the holder of its highest office accountable. This exercise is rooted in her moral compass and her willingness to act as American democracy's mother, loving, stern, and resolute. Her integrity and courage were vital to being able to call out the wrongdoings within the Nixon administration because she saw it as a threat to democracy. Jordan had plenty of experience in defying the odds, coming from Texas and having been in plenty of spaces no other Black woman had trod. She, like a mother, was certain to call out the offenses committed, yet did her best to protect the delicate democracy that she held so dear.

# CHAPTER 3

## *Building on the Foundation*

The foundational women of the CBC provided a blueprint for how Black women could be successful legislators by pushing the American democracy. Their push was about actualizing the rights gained through the judiciary and the legislature in the 1960s and 1970s. This actualization provided a voice for the voiceless even though these women were largely legislatively insignificant. By being the first Black women in these roles, they cemented their presence as descriptive legislators unafraid of the complex legislative apparatus. Their radical imaginations first asserted that they deserved to be representatives in the U.S. House. This in turn normalized their presence in a legislative body that was founded while the larger society categorized them as property. Moreover, they cemented the idea that the CBC worked as agents for people who cannot speak for themselves. This is best exemplified in a statement made by Maxine Waters, a representative from California's 43rd district:

> ...even though the public does not know what you have prevented you know it is your responsibility whether people know what you are doing or even care about what you are doing you know it's your responsibility to avoid the constituents and the consumers of this country from getting ripped off, from being undermined, from being taken advantage of... (*Who Am I*, 2019)

Maxine Waters, Barbara-Rose Collins, and Eleanor Holmes Norton usher in a new era for the women of the CBC. These three women from different corners of the country were poised to expand the gains procured by the foundational women of the CBC (Table 3.1).

Table 3.1  Congressional Black Caucus Key Female Foundation Builder

| Foundation Builder | State and Congressional District | Congressional Terms and Years Served | Total Number of Bills Sponsored | Total Number of Bills Cosponsored |
|---|---|---|---|---|
| Maxine Waters | California's 29th district | 102nd (1991–1993) | 578 | 4,557 |
| | 35th district | 103rd–112th (1993–2013) | | |
| | 43rd district | 113th–119th (2013–present) | | |
| Eleanor Holmes Norton | District of Columbia | 102nd–119th (1991–present) | 1,036 | 15,643 |
| Carrie Meek | Florida 17th district | 103rd–107th (1993–2003) | 62 | 1,766 |
| Eddie Bernice Johnson | Texas 30th district | 103rd–117th (1993–2023) | 347 | 5,691 |

There is a 9-year gap between the election of Representative Katie Hall of Indiana's first district and the election of Maxine Waters of California's 29th district. These years fall squarely inside of the Reagan Administration, which birthed Reaganomics. Reaganomics is the economic policy that was implemented by the Reagan Administration with the intention to reduce government spending, reduce capital gains tax and federal income tax, reduce company regulation and lower the money supply in an attempt to lower inflation, lower the unemployment rate, create more jobs, and overall expand the economy (Ronald Reagan Presidential Foundation & Institute). As part of lowering government spending, funding for departments like Agriculture, Commerce, Housing and Urban Development, as well as the Department of Labor were cut. Spending cuts even included Republican-cherished enclaves like the Department of Defense. The Department saw a 5.7% cut, which was equivalent to $44 billion (St. Pierre, 1991). Over half of the budget reduction came from these areas: income security; and education, training, employment and social services. The constituents who were to absorb such devastating federal divestment were the poor, who were often Black.

Blacks suffered disproportionately from the Reagan programs because a higher proportion of Blacks during the 1980s were poorer than Whites. The net employment increase for Blacks in the public sector was 55% before the Reagan Administration. Therefore, reductions in social welfare programs caused a higher percentage of Blacks than Whites to lose their jobs (St. Pierre, 1991). Programs like Food Stamps, which disproportionately affected Black households, changed instituting work in the next 30 days' mandates, which was severely limiting aid. The loss of this aid during the Reagan Administration was compounded because 56% of Blacks lived in central cities. Only around 20% of Blacks lived in the suburbs, making them far more vulnerable to Reagan spending cuts. In addition, the average Black family income was $15,432 compared with $27,686 for White families during the administration. The harm done to Blacks in the Reagan Administration was evident as 50% of Black males between the ages of 16 and 19 became unemployed. This is coupled with the overall Black unemployment at 15.2% compared with 6.2% for Whites (U.S. Bureau of Labor Statistics).

Therefore, when Waters, Collins, and Holmes Norton joined the House of Representatives in 1991 for the 102nd Congress, they were prepared to restore Black communities. Eleanor Holmes Norton, a civil rights activist, 1964 Yale School of Law graduate and native of Washington, DC, was no stranger to the plight of Blacks across the country. President Jimmy Carter appointed Norton as the chair of the U.S. Equal Employment Opportunity Commission in 1977; she became the first female head of the agency. Norton's extensive understanding of federal civil rights laws helped her establish the first set of regulations outlining what constituted sexual harassment, while declaring that sexual harassment was indeed a form of sexual discrimination. Her visibility in this role undoubtedly played a role in her joining the Georgetown University Law Center in 1982.

As a young Black woman who came of age during the height of Jim and Jane Crow laws, Black self-determination has consistently been at the forefront of Norton's consciousness. Washington, DC, was nicknamed "Chocolate City," shortly after the passage of the District of Columbia's Home Rule Act in 1973. The primary Black city had suffered mightily under the Reagan Administration and needed financial assistance. Congresswoman Holmes Norton help to end the city's most serious financial crisis by achieving a historic package that restructured the financial relationship between Congress and the District, by transferring $5 billion in unfunded pension liabilities and billions more in state costs to the federal government (Environmental Law Institute, n.d.). This allowed Black mayors Marion Berry and Sharon Pratt Kelley to right the financial ship in a territory where Blacks did not have the protection of statehood.

Congresswoman Norton's fight for DC statehood has persisted in her 32-year career in the House of Representatives. Norton is only the second delegate to represent Washington, DC, after Walter Fauntroy. Because Washington, DC, is not a state, neither Fauntroy nor Norton was a voting member in the House. This legislative function makes Congresswoman Horton invisible because her voting record is nonexistent. Yet, this has not stopped her advocacy and she is responsible for H.R. 4361 (103rd): Federal Employees Family Friendly Leave Act; H.R. 2017 (104th): 1995 DC Emergency Highway Relief Act; H.R. 1499 (107th): District of Columbia College Access Improvement Act of 2002; and H.R. 866 (116th) 2019: Fairness for Breastfeeding Mothers.

The Federal Employees Family Friendly Leave Act authorizes employees to use a total of up to 40 hr of sick leave per year to care for family members and bereavement, and extended the maximum hours for family care to 104 hr per year. The ability to care for families and loved ones can be directly attributed to the Congresswoman's experiences as a Black woman. The invisible labor of caretaking is societally attributed to women. In the case of Black women who are often the breadwinners for their families, the need to caretake can produce an uncomfortable decision. This law was signed in 1994 while Black women were ascending to new heights in a variety of industries thought to be out of their reach. This legislation benefits a great and diverse group of people, but Congresswoman Norton understands that this will specifically help Black women.

Norton keenly understands that the ability for Black women to achieve career advancement, climb the ladder of success, and not have to sacrifice their family in the process was tied into this legislation.

The District of Columbia College Access Improvement Act of 2002 was designed to expand the options for students seeking higher education. Congresswoman Norton's time in Congress taught her, as it did to many other CBC members, that amending previous legislation proved to provide the greatest legislative success. The improvement act was designed to amend the District of Columbia College Access Act of 1999, which allowed DC high school students the ability to pay in-state tuition at state colleges across the country. This leveraged the lack of DC statehood as the original college access act asserted the lack of state higher education choices. It was an innovative way to help her Black constituents choose state Historically Black Universities without paying absorbent out-of-state fees.

Her intentions were even clearer with the improvement, as it allowed individuals to enroll in higher education institutions more than 3 years after graduating from a secondary school. It also expanded the pool of institutions who could participate in the tuition assistance programs to private HBCUs nationwide. With noted higher education divestment by state governments and the legacy of HBCU graduates creating the Black middle class, Norton's legislation carved out a path for her constituents. The improvement act allows Black constituents in her district to take advantage of extending their education without having to enact brand new legislation, while strengthening the infrastructure of HBCUs.

Barbara-Rose Collins of Michigan's 13th district was known as an advocate for the Black community. She was the first Black woman from Michigan to be elected to Congress, and like many of the foundational female CBC members served in her state's legislature. Yet, Collins was no stranger to serving in a political capacity; she was a member of the Detroit Public School Board from 1971 to 1973, and a member of the Detroit City Council from 1982 to 1991, where she returned after her brief 6-year stint in the House (Rahal, 2021). During her tenure, only one of the 27 resolutions she sponsored became law: H.R. 4967 (103rd): To designate the Federal building and U.S. courthouse in Detroit, Michigan, as the "Theodore Levin Federal Building and United States Courthouse."

On June 17, 2021, President Joe Biden signed the Juneteenth National Independence Day Act, which was sponsored by Senator Edward J. Markey of Massachusetts (Wagner, 2021). However, Barbara-Rose Collins was the first to sponsor a bill; H.J.Res. 195 Recognizing the end of slavery in the United States, recognized as the true day of independence for African Americans. After her success with a piece of symbolic legislation in the 103rd for the Jewish community, she tried to gain a symbolic victory for Blacks. She, along with the help of the members of the CBC, got the legislation to pass the House, but the legislation died in Senate. The confidence she had to sponsor a major piece of legislation that would require the United States to acknowledge slavery in a formalized way is remarkable. The consciousness of a woman from Michigan miles away from Galveston, TX, to consider the collective may have played a role in the loss of her seat.

Maxine Waters is undoubtedly one the most influential Black women in the history of the House of Representatives and the CBC. She is a native of St. Louis, MO, but moved to Los Angeles, CA, in the early 1960s. She was elected to the California State Assembly in 1976 and worked on the divestment of state pension funds from any businesses active in South Africa operating under the policy of apartheid (Waters, 2008). She occupied the seat of Augustus "Gus" Freeman Hawkins, a native of Shreveport Louisiana, who was a founding member of the CBC affectionately known as the mighty 13.

Congresswoman Waters started her 17th term in the House during the 118th Congress. She embodies the "Unbought and Unbossed" spirit of Shirley Chisolm. As a California state legislature for 7 years, she was able to mimic the House of Representatives before she served in the federal legislature. She is the most senior of the 13 Black women serving in Congress and chaired the CBC from 1997 to 1999. She is the second-most senior member of the California congressional delegation, after Nancy Pelosi. She chaired the House Financial Services Committee from 2019 to 2023 and has been the ranking member since 2023 (Waters, 2024).

Waters has consistently been a Black voice of resistance. From the Los Angeles riots during the Rodney King verdict to the Derek Chauvin trial, Congresswoman Waters is visible in the Black community and is being seen as the larger community's "auntie" who will tell the truth indiscriminate of the unfavorable repercussions. Yet, this heroic stance does not come without risk: on October 24, 2018, packages containing a pipe bomb were sent to two of Waters' offices. However, the vigilance of the Federal Bureau of Investigation intercepted the packages and arrested the suspect.

However, the threats to her political power come from all directions. Citizens for Responsibility and Ethics in Washington, a nonpartisan non-profit organization founded in 2003 committed to holding those who abuse the system to be accountable, named Waters to its list of corrupt members of Congress in its 2005, 2006, 2009, and 2011 reports (CREW, 2024). These reports triggered a review by the Ethics Committee in the House of Representatives. There was a 3-year investigation into her and her husband's involvement with OneUnited Bank that received federal aid. In September 2008, during the subprime mortgage crisis that affected global markets, Waters arranged meetings between U.S. Treasury Department officials and OneUnited Bank. The bank heavily invested in Freddie Mac and Fannie Mae and desperately needed a cash infusion. The bank received $12 million through the Troubled Asset Relief Program money (Crabtree, 2016). Waters was charged with violations of the House's ethics rules because her husband was a shareholder at the bank. Yet, on September 21, 2012, the House Ethics Committee cleared Waters of all ethics charges.

Congresswoman Waters' commitment to radical legislative action has resulted in only 9 of her 402 pieces of legislation being signed into law. Yet, two of those nine were sponsored in the 117th Congress as a result of the COVID pandemic: H.R. 1724 and H.R. 1725. H.R. 1724 provided additional funding inside of fiscal year 2021 for emergency rental assistance vouchers through the Department of Housing and Urban Development. This legislation was designed to help families and individuals who were experiencing homelessness, at risk of homelessness: recently homeless, and fleeing, or attempting to flee, domestic violence, and other dangerous situations. Congresswoman Waters understood the housing insecurities that existed in her district, but better understood that COVID-19 placed many Black families and Black people in survival mode. The expansion of federal funding for the already-established programs allowed for more people to receive the assistance they needed from their government in a time of economic uncertainty.

In the 117th Congress, Waters also sponsored H.R. 1725, which was passed into law. This bill established the blueprint for rental assistance and moratorium exercised throughout the country during the COVID-19 pandemic. This Act like the previous provides additional funding for the Department of the Treasury's Emergency Rental Assistance program during fiscal year 2021. The program, established in response to the COVID-19 pandemic, provides grants to states, local governments, and territories for financial assistance to households for rent, utilities, and other housing expenses. The period of assistance was capped at 18 months. Congresswoman Waters has proven to be a formidable force in the House of Representatives and within the CBC.

After Collins, Norton, and Waters entered the House of Representatives, Black women in southern states began to see the benefits of the Civil Rights Act of 1965 with redistricting caused by the 1990 census. In 1992 and 1993, five more women joined the CBC: Eva Clayton of North Carolina's 1st district who served from 1992 to 2002; Corrine Brown of Florida's 3rd and 5th district who served from 1993 to 2017; Eddie Bernice Johnson of Texas' 30th district who served from 1993 to 2022; Cynthia McKinney of Georgia's 4th and 11th districts who served from 1993 to 2007; and Carrie Meek of Florida's 17th district who served from 1993 to 2003. This growth in the Caucus caused friction as differing interest from across the country and differing personalities began to rub against one another.

On July 29, 1994, during the highly partisan Whitewater hearings, Maxine Waters asserted her authority (C-SPAN, 1994). She repeatedly interrupted a speech by Peter King, a Republican of New York's 3rd district after he badgered Margaret Williams. Ms. Williams was the first Black woman to be the Chief of Staff to the First Lady, Hillary Rodman Clinton. The presiding officer, fellow CBC member Carrie Meek classed her behavior as "unruly and turbulent," and threatened to have the Sergeant at Arms present her with the Mace of the House of Representatives. Yet, Waters was unfazed and the *Los Angeles Times* reported her saying, "Women are new to this place. Women are supposed to know their place. I exercise my rights and it's new for men. It's not easy for them to accept women as equal partners" (Bornemeier, 1994).

However, the differing of legislative styles did not stop these women of the new southern block, from being concerned about those they came to Congress to descriptively represent. Therefore, the following discussion will highlight the legislation these ladies sponsored that became law. It is to display visible impact to the Black community although unrecognized or seen as marginal by the larger legislative apparatus. In the 105th Congress, Eva Clayton of North Carolina's 1st district sponsored H.R. 2796 Army Reserve-National Guard Equity Reimbursement Act, which was passed into law. The act authorized the reimbursement of members of the Army deployed to Europe in support of operations in Bosnia. The legislation was targeted to provide reimbursements for certain out-of-pocket expenses incurred. In 1995, nearly a quarter of the Army was Black and many of them were deployed in a peacekeeping mission in Bosnia (Baumann et al., 2024; Staff, 2024). National Guard service members were not at parity with active-duty soldiers something Clayton knew about being the first African American to represent North Carolina. This piece of legislation targeted those who were in greater need financially, which were undoubtedly Black people.

In the 107th Congress, Cynthia McKinney of Georgia and Carrie Meek of Florida passed two pieces of legislation, which speaks of the history of racism in the country. Each of the Acts have regional significance, which furthers the argument of visibility in the Black community. These bills show an understanding of the legislative process while producing substantive legislation that solidified the legacy of Blacks in America. Of the 124 bills these women collectively sponsored, only three became law. This speaks to the difficulty of getting legislation passed into law, but a review of each of these women's legislative records would show a clear sign of legislative activism. McKinney sponsored H.R. 2261, which became law making the U.S. Postal Service located at 2853 Candler Road in Decatur, GA, the "Earl T. Shinhoster Post Office." Shinhoster was a civil rights activist who had attended Morehouse College and spent 30 years working with the NAACP. Congresswoman Cynthia McKinney was the daughter of Billy McKinney a long-time member of the Georgia House of Representatives, and one of Atlanta's first Black police officers. She knew this legislation would mean a great deal to Blacks in Atlanta who were actualizing opportunities afforded by Shinhoster's and other's work. More substantially, the naming of this post office would force the American psyche to contend with Shinhoster and the necessity of his work with his name on a federal building.

Carrie Meek was the first African American since the Reconstruction era elected to represent Florida. It is important again to note that without sections four and five of the Civil Rights Act of 1965, her election would not be possible. A review of her legislative record would also show a commitment of legislative activism, which was taken up by her son Kendrick Meek, who served the same district, once she vacated the seat after serving for 10 years. In the 107th Congress, Congresswoman Meek sponsored H.R. 2109 which was signed into law and authorized a special resource study of Virginia Key Beach Park. The study was done by the Secretary of the Interior for the park's possible inclusion in the National Park System.

As a visible and active member of her community, Congresswoman Meek was aware of the history of Miami inside of Dade County Florida. The City of Miami was founded in 1896 after the end of Reconstruction in 1877. One-third of the cities chartering signatures came from Black men who played a predominant role in the early building of the city. Yet, by the 1920s a system of Jim Crow laws had been firmly established that se intern developed Miami-Dade County beaches into parks with public swimming facilities exclusively for Whites. Therefore, Dana Dorsey, a Black millionaire at the time, purchased Fisher Island so that Blacks could have a beach of their own. He was later forced to sell the property through the increase in property taxes to Miami Beach Pioneer Carl Fisher in the 1940s (Tester, 2024).

In June 1999, citizens called the Virginia Key Beach Park Civil Rights Task Force united to address the potential private development on the beach park, and Congresswoman Meek was engaged. She understood that the larger municipality needed money to reopen the beach after years of neglect, and inclusion of Virginia Key Beach, once named Fisher Island, in the National Park System would provide the needed resources. Although the beach was not added to the National Park System, the study resulted in the location's addition to the National Register of Historic Places in August 2002. Subsequently, the historic Virginia Key

Beach Park reopened to the public in February 2008. Congresswoman Meek's understanding of legislative process and willingness to use the process to protect the legacy of Blacks aligns with Dowe's argument about the Black women who run for office. Meek understood her role as a culture carrier, which is evident in sponsored legislation H.R. 2109 and passing the legislative baton to her son.

Corrine Brown of Florida and Eddie Bernice Johnson of Texas were the last female additions to the CBC during this era of southern expansion. Congresswoman Brown sponsored H.R. 2447 in the 112th Congress, which authorized a Congressional Gold Medal to collectively honor the Montford Point Marines. Camp Montford Point, NC, was the site for the training of the first Black Marines who served during the World War II, and their contributions in key battles had not been recognized. Yet, her work with honoring the contributions of Blacks in the military was largely overshadowed by a federal indictment concerning the nonprofit charity One Door for Education Foundation. Allegedly, the charity was designed to provide scholarships to underprivileged students, but instead was a personal slush fund for Brown and her associates.

On May 11, 2017, Brown was convicted on 18 of 22 corruption charges ranging from mail fraud to filing a false federal tax return. On December 4, 2017, she was sentenced to 5 years in prison and ordered to pay restitution; yet, on May 6, 2021, the conviction was overturned. The 11th Circuit Court of Appeals decided that a juror had been improperly removed by the trial judge, which ultimately decided the case. After 2 years in prison, Brown chose to avoid a new trial and on May 17, 2022, plead guilty to the charge of interference with the due administration of IRS laws with time served (Saunders et al., 2021).

Corrine Brown is an example of the high scrutiny Black legislators face when inside of the federal legislature. The Florida A&M University rattler, a historically Black university in Florida created due to the discrimination at Florida State, was unafraid to strike inside of the legislature. She openly objected to Florida's 25 electoral college votes being given to George W. Bush in the 2000 election. She voted no on the Electronic Surveillance Modernization Act and voted no on the Military Commissions Act, both pieces of legislation crafted in the name of winning the War on Terror. Yet, she understood that each of these laws would undoubtedly hurt Black Americans. However, her trust in long-time employee Elias "Ronnie" Simmons and her ignorance and lack of understanding for IRS rules concerning nonprofit charities ensured her political demise.

Brown's experiences are a modern-day cautionary tale concerning visibility and invisibility. Black people, and especially Black women, are invisible until malfeasance makes you visible. Like Maxine Waters, Shelia Jackson Lee, and Barbara Lee, Corrine Brown became visible once she was unwilling to be complicit in governmental action that erodes democracy. Brown like each of the other women listed understood how the myth of White Supremacy allows for the justification of unchecked absolute power. Any rebuke or unauthorized use of these women's political agency must be checked. In Brown's case, her inability to fiercely monitor the activities of her nonprofit, indiscriminate of her intentions provided the insidious tool required to quench her political power.

Eddie Bernice Johnson of Texas' 30th district has a long and historic career spending 29 years in the House of Representative sponsoring 311 bills, yet only five became law. Congresswoman Johnson like many other women of the CBC served in her state legislature of Texas; however, her tenure was special as she served in both the state house and Senate. Throughout her political career she worked against racism and sexism. Thomas Korosec of the Chicago Tribune publishes a story "Eyes on Texas: Where Men are Men and Women Run for Public Office" on August 19, 1990, and quotes her saying "Being a woman and being Black is perhaps a double handicap … when you see who's in the important huddles, who's making the important decisions, it's men" (*Star-Telegram*, 2021).

Congresswoman Johnson left the Texas State House in 1977, when President Jimmy Carter appointed her as the regional director for the Department of Health, Education, and Welfare, and she was the first Black woman in this position (The HistoryMakers, n.d.). Eddie Bernice Johnson was an excellent choice for this role as a nurse who spent 20 years in the profession before entering politics. Moreover, Johnson was accustomed to being the first; she was the first Black person as well as the first Black woman to serve as Chief Psychiatric Nurse at the Dallas

Veterans Administration Hospital. In December 2010, Johnson became the first Black person as well as the first female ranking member of the House Committee on Science, Space, and Technology, and in 2019 went on to become the chairwoman for that committee.

Congresswoman Johnson was a leader among leaders serving as the 17th chairwoman of the CBC from 2001 to 2003. She, like Corrine Brown, objected to Florida giving George W. Bush their 25 electoral college votes. In fact, Chairwoman Johnson led the Black Caucus out of the House chamber in January 2001 when Congress met for its ceremonial certification of the electoral college victory (Livingston & Salhotra, 2023).

She was consistently a champion for the least of these with her sponsoring of H.R. 6618 the Stop Deceptive Advertising of Gas Prices Act or her sponsorship of H.R. 5586 Expanding Tax Assistance Act of 2008, after the subprime mortgage collapse that disproportionately affected Blacks maintaining ownership of their homes.

Yet, her advocacy for Blacks was far more implicit with her sponsorship of H.R. 692 Racial Equity and Fair Treatment Act of 2003. The legislation would authorize the Secretary of Health and Human Services to award grants to States in an effort to support programs for low-income families with children. In particular, it would require:

> interpretation and translation services for TANF recipients; an expedited process for discrimination complaints; a provision regarding TANF recipients right and training for program personnel in respecting such rights; along with an opportunity for TANF applicants or recipients to appeal adverse decisions. (H.R. 692)

Unsurprisingly, this bill died in committee and did not reach the House Floor for a vote. Yet, in the 116th Congress Johnson sponsored H.R. 1396 Hidden Figures Congressional Gold Medal Act, which passed and became law even after a 40-min debate surrounding its passage on the House Floor.

H.R. 1396 awarded Congressional Gold Medals to Katherine Johnson and Dr. Christine Darden, and posthumously to Dorothy Vaughan and Mary Jackson who contributed to the success of the National Aeronautics and Space Administration during the Space Race. These women were named in Disney's *Hidden Figures*, a biographical drama film directed loosely based on their contributions in the Space Race some 60 years prior. This motion picture was based upon Margot Lee Shetterly's (2016), a Black woman, nonfiction book, *Hidden Figures: The American Dream and the Untold Story of the Black Women Who Helped Win the Space Race*. The bill was careful not to ignore other Black women who might forever be inviable and awarded a Congressional Gold Medal to all the unnamed women who contributed. Although viewed as legislatively insignificant, this legislation cemented three things: The invisible work that Black women do which changes the world around them; the fight to become visible with the prolonged process to be recognized by the American government 3 years after the motion picture; and the fact that Black women are always required to make those who are invisible visible again.

# CHAPTER 4

## Expanding the Collective

After the era of southern expansion, the CBC was becoming too powerful, growing from the original 13 members at the start of the 92nd Congress. In the 103rd Congress, Republicans were the minority with only 176 seats, yet in the 104th Congress they gained 54 seats giving them a majority over Democrats who had 203 seats to Republicans' 230. This allowed for Republican Newt Gingrich, the representative from Georgia's 6th district, to become the new Speaker of the House. The Republican Party, during the midterm elections in the first term of President Clinton, ran on a platform of smaller government. When Congressman Gingrich became the speaker, he brought about sweeping changes in an effort to produce that smaller government.

These changes were captured in a *New York Times* article by Michael Wines written on December 8, 1994, entitled "Republicans Seek Sweeping Changes in House Rules" (Nelson, 2022). It was clear that these changes were designed to reduce the proliferation of racial caucuses, while simultaneously reducing the number of House committees. Although the CBC members did not have a numerical advantage, they were gaining tenure and becoming ranking members. Privileges provided in the House of Representatives are tied to longevity as the body is four times that of the Senate. Those privileges include being chairmen and chairwomen of committees. This thought was untenable for many in the chamber and changes needed to be made. It is important to note that

Gingrich just delayed the inevitable. By the 111th Congress, the CBC had saturated all the 22 standing committees and three of their male members were Chairs.

Gingrich may have thwarted the efforts of the CBC for a season, but that only ignited a fire under the fresh Black women legislators who joined the House. It was during his speakership that the following women became members of the CBC: Sheila Jackson Lee of Texas' 18th district, Juanita Millender-McDonald of California's 37th district, Carolyn Cheeks Kilpatrick of Michigan's 15th district, Donna Christian-Christensen a new nonvoting member from the Virgin Islands, Julia Carson of Indiana's 10th and later 7th districts, and Barbara Lee of California's 9th, 13th, and 12th districts.

The two women who open and close this era have 30-year legislative careers in the House of Representatives: Sheila Jackson Lee served from 1995 until her death on July 19, 2024, and Barbara Lee from 1998 to 2025. Congresswoman Jackson Lee is known in legislative circles for her legislative fight for reparations. Jackson Lee picked up the mantle leading the effort for the creation of a commission to study reparations for African Americans after CBC member John Conyers. John Conyers is the longest serving Black member of Congressional history at 52 years (Nelson, 2022). In 1989, he sponsored the Commission to Study and Develop Reparation Proposals for African-Americans Act. After his retirement in 2017, Congresswoman Jackson Lee sponsored the bill every session believing she had the votes in the 117th Congress before her death.

Sponsorship of this bill in each legislative session was seen as irrational along with many other of the 722 bills she sponsored. Legislation like H.R. 2116 Creating a Respectful and Open World for Natural Hair Act of 2022 or H.R. 750 Save America Comprehensive Immigration Act of 2007 was seen as too far outside of the American imagination. The latter Act was authored during the George W. Bush administration and aligned with their policy initiatives. Yet, Congresswoman Jackson Lee was not the administration's chosen messenger. The Congresswoman was known to be direct and often found herself visible in the media catching strong ire for not acting like a lady (Digital, 2023). Yet, as a girl born in Queens,

NY, who graduated with a Bachelor of Arts in political science from Yale University in 1972, aggressive behavior was the norm.

Sheila Jackson Lee had an extraordinary legislative career sponsoring 722 bills, serving on the Judiciary Committee, Homeland Security Committee, and the Committee on Budget. Yet, only 11 of her 722 bills became law. Her lengthy career and forthright negotiation style presented a natural fit as the Whip of the Congressional Black Caucus; she often gathered the votes necessary for CBC initiatives. She moved to Houston in 1987 to establish roots after graduating from the University of Virginia School of Law in 1975. In 1989, Jackson Lee was elected to the Houston City Council, where she served in the office until 1994 (Govindarao, 2024). To win Texas' 18th district, she first had to defeat incumbent Craig Washington; she seized the political moment and showed the district she was the advocate they were looking for. Congresswoman Jackson Lee died in July 2024, and on November 12, 2024, Erica Lee Carter, her daughter, was sworn in to finish her term (Page, 2024). This made history as the first mother and daughter to succeed each other in the U.S. legislature. After the death of Sheila Jackson Lee, President Biden, a long-time congressional colleague, said, "She was unrelenting in her leadership" (Lozano, 2024).

Congresswoman Jackson Lee opposed a guest worker program, but championed border security and increasing opportunities for legalization. In 2001, Jackson Lee objected to counting Florida's electoral votes for George W. Bush. In 2002, she voted against the Authorization for Use of Military Force Against Iraq Resolution that authorized the Iraq War. In 2003, Jackson Lee advocated for changing the names of tropical cyclones and hurricanes to be inclusive of African American names. In 2009, she voted for the Matthew Shepard and James Byrd Jr. Hate Crimes Prevention Act, a bill that expanded the federal hate crime law to cover crimes biased by the victim's sexual orientation or gender identity. Jackson Lee opposed repealing the Patient Protection and Affordable Care Act known as Obama Care multiple times.

During the COVID-19 pandemic, Jackson Lee brought United Airlines to task as they have a hub at Houston's George Bush International Airport. The airline had accepted billions of dollars in taxpayer funds through the

CARES Act and the Paycheck Protection Program, yet still threaten to furlough workers (Price, 2023). In August 2022, Jackson Lee voted for the Inflation Reduction Act to help Americans after the pandemic. Jackson Lee was one of three Democrats that abstained from voting in the formal censure of Congresswoman Rashida Talib, which was proposed by Republican Rich McCormick. She proved to be just what President Biden called her unrelenting.

Her advocacy and the protection of democracy is best seen in these two pieces of legislation, which became law, H.R. 6610 in the 110th Congress and H.R. 4696 in the 118th Congress. H.R. 6610 was concerned with the Federal Rules of Evidence. Congresswoman Jackson Lee as a trained lawyer understood that what was admissible in trial and what wasn't, and played a large role in convictions. Therefore, she sought to amend the protections of those brought up on charges by the federal government by amending the waiver of the attorney–client privilege and the work product doctrine and by amending the Federal Rules of Evidence with respect to the disclosure of a communication or information covered by the attorney–client privilege, and work product protection. This legislation has proven to be quite substantial as it amends the evidence that can be accepted in the federal indictments of Donald Trump.

Congresswoman Jackson Lee's protection of American democracy is also seen in H.R. 4696. The Foreign Extortion Prevention Act amended title 18 of the U.S. Code to prohibit a foreign official from demanding a bribe, and extortion for other purposes. Although the congresswoman did not sit on the Foreign Affairs Committee, she was well versed in foreign affairs. She was vocal about the United States' role in counter-insurgency operations in Venezuela as well as the United States' relations with Iran and Cuba. She traveled to Azerbaijan at their government's expense. Therefore, she was familiar with the need to have clear guardrails codified in legislation to ensure government officials were not extorted.

Juanita Millender-McDonald of California's 37th district, Carolyn Cheeks Kilpatrick of Michigan's 13th and 15th districts, and Julia Carson of Indiana's 10th district were successful in getting legislation passed that protected Black identity across the country. In the 106th Congress, Carson sponsored H.R. 573, which authorized then President

Clinton to award a gold medal to Rosa Parks in recognition of her contributions to the nation. This attribution was furthered in the 109th by Congresswoman Cheeks Kilpatrick. H.R. 2967 designated the federal building located at 333 Mt. Elliott Street in Detroit, MI, as the "Rosa Parks Federal Building." Rosa Parks' bold acts in Montgomery, AL, were well known in the Black community but tacit in the American psyche. The legislative careers of each of these women are directly connected to Parks putting her life on the line in the name of equality. Although Rosa's actions benefited the entire nation, Black women were necessary to make her contributions visible.

Congresswomen Juanita Millender-McDonald sponsored H.R. 5157 in the 106th Congress. The Freedmen's Bureau Records Preservation Act of 2000 directed archivist to preserve the records of the Bureau of Refugees, Freedmen, and Abandoned Lands. The legislation authorized federal funds to use microfilm technology to preserve these records. The Act was a result of a pilot project with the University of Florida alongside Howard University. The legislation is evidence of Millender-McDonald's understanding of the inequities between Predominate White Institutions and HBCUs. The appropriations were careful to ensure that funding was steered toward HBCUs who had and still have treasure troves of archival material. The indexing of these records and making them more easily accessible to the public allow historians and genealogists the ability to tell competing historical narratives about the Reconstruction period in America.

Congresswoman Donna Christian-Christensen, the nonvoting member from Virgin Islands, got two pieces of legislation passed, which helped the island with their own self-determination, which increased their autonomy. H.R. 6116 in the 112th Congress and H.R. 83 in the 113th Congress allowed the Virgin Islands more autonomy in governing themselves. H.R. 6116 amended the Revised Organic Act of the Virgin Islands. The legislation removed the temporary jurisdiction of the U.S. Court of Appeals for the Third Circuit established in the Organic Act. Before the passage of this Act, the U.S. Supreme Court could review, by a writ of certiorari, the final decisions of the highest court of the Virgin Islands. This ultimately allowed the U.S. judicial system to be the final arbitrator of judicial decisions that reached the Virgin Island's Supreme Court.

Conceptually, this would mean that a group of predominately White judges would be able to overturn the decisions of a group of predominately Black judges. The Congresswoman's understanding shifted this reality giving the island final say in judicial matters.

Delegate Christian-Christensen went further in the 113th Congress with the Consolidated and Further Continuing Appropriations Act, 2015. She used this Act to increase funding, while directing funding in different areas across the island. The Act increased total funding above Fiscal Year 2014 levels by combining the following legislation: Agriculture, Rural Development, Food and Drug Administration, and Related Agencies Appropriations Act, 2015; the Energy and Water Development and Related Agencies Appropriations Act, 2015; the Department of Labor, Health, and Human Services, and Education, and Related Agencies Appropriations Act, 2015; the Legislative Branch Appropriations Act, 2015; the Military Construction and Veterans Affairs, and Related Agencies Appropriations Act, 2015; the Department of State, Foreign Operations, and Related Programs Appropriations Act, 2015; and the Transportation, Housing and Urban Development, and Related Agencies Appropriations Act, 2015. The legislation subsequently decreased funding in areas that would have provided more federal oversight through the Department of Defense Appropriations Act, 2015 and the Department of the Interior, Environment, and Related Agencies Appropriations Act, 2015.

This legislation took time to maturate through the congressional process. The bill was originally introduced on January 3, 2013, by Delegate Donna Christian-Christensen. She used her influence as a committee member on the House Transportation and Infrastructure regarding clean energy in insular areas. The bill passed in the House on September 15, 2014, and the Senate on September 18, 2014, but the Senate made some changes. However, those changes did not substantially change the aim of the legislation. The bill was signed into law by President Obama on December 16, 2014, providing the island a notable Christmas present. Delegate Christian-Christensen used her understanding of the legislative structure to bring about meaningful change. She was patient allowing the legislation to move through both Houses of Congress with a total of 66 legislative actions. It is undeniable that frustrations built along the way, especially as a nonvoting member, but she understood that this shift in funding would fundamentally change the governance and growth possibilities on the island. Her use of that process provided a funding structure that has allowed the island to be self-sufficient in the judicial, legislative, and executive governance structure.

Barbara Lee of California's 9th, 13th, and now 12th district was the last Black female CBC member elected during the Newt Gingrich era. She won a special election after the resignation of Ronald Dellums, one of the original CBC members. She, like many of her female colleagues, knew what it meant to be first as she was the first Black woman to represent northern California in the state legislature in both state houses. Congresswoman Lee followed in her predecessors' ideological footsteps voting as the House of Representatives most liberal Democrat in the 111th Congress (Nelson, 2022, p. 57). It was also in the 111th Congress that Congresswoman Lee was elected as the Chairwoman for the CBC. Her service in CBC leadership aligned with the commencement of the Obama Administration. He had taken a strong stance on troop reduction in the Middle East, and Congresswomen Lee came to national attention because of a historic vote concerning the war.

On September 18, 2001, the Authorization for Use of Military Force Against Terrorists (AUMF) became law, but that was after Congresswoman Lee who was the only member of Congress to vote against. As a member of the legislature who understood her constitutional role to declare war, she opposed the military action because she believed it granted the president overly broad powers to wage war. Lee understood that by being the lone nonsupporter of the bill her decision looked irrational. Therefore, on September 23, 2001, she wrote an opinion piece in the *San Francisco Gate* and stated the legislation:

> ....was a blank check to the president to attack anyone involved in the September 11 events—anywhere, in any country, without regard to our nation's long-term foreign policy, economic and national security interests, and without time limit. In granting these overly broad powers, the Congress failed its responsibility to understand the dimensions of its declaration. I could not support such a grant of war-making authority to the president; I believe it would put more innocent lives at risk. The president has the constitutional authority to protect the nation from further attack, and he has mobilized the armed forces to do just that. The Congress should have waited for the facts to be presented and then acted with fuller knowledge of the consequences of our action. (Lee, 2001)

It was in this piece that she acknowledged the influx of calls that tied up her switchboard on Capitol Hill due to her decision to vote against. Capitol Police provided round-the-clock bodyguards due to the death threats against her and her family.

Congresswoman Lee's congressional career has been filled with liberal stances that drew attention to issues of the least of these. Lee has repeated over her career the impact Shirley Chisolm had on her life and the causes she felt responsible to further. Lee is the author of H.R. 176: Shirley A. Chisholm United States-Caribbean Educational Exchange Act of 2008 in the 110th Congress. The bill died in committee but would have enhanced U.S. foreign relations with CARICOM nations, while using the United States Agency for International Development to develop programing that would strengthen education and increased community involvement in school activities. Her commitment to the least of these included the environment that was displayed in H.R. 4932: Women and Climate Change Act of 2018. As a single mother for the majority of her career, she was keen to the needs of women, understanding women make up the majority of the world's poor. Subsequently, abrupt changes in the environment due to climate change left many women, as the leaders in their families, to find food and clean water, and secure safe housing for loved ones.

As a Congresswoman from California, Lee has been a front runner in the reformation of cannabis laws in Congress. Each of the following pieces of legislation seeks to correct injustices around the criminalization of cannabis and its disproportionate effect on Black communities. She was an original cosponsor of H.R. 2306: Ending Federal Marijuana Prohibition Act of 2011 with Congressman Barney Frank of Massachusetts' 4th district. In the 114th Congress, she sponsored H.R. 262: States' Medical Marijuana Property Rights Protection Act. In the 116th Congress, she sponsored H.R. 1455: Restraining Excessive Federal Enforcement & Regulations of Cannabis Act of 2019 and H.R. 1456: Marijuana Justice Act of 2019. In the 118th Congress, she sponsored H.R. 2682: Veterans Medical Marijuana Safe Harbor Act and H.Res. 960: Realizing Equitable & Sustainable Participation in Emerging Cannabis Trades (RESPECT) Resolution.

All this legislation built on the Marijuana Justice Act to remove cannabis from the Controlled Substances Act. The removal would fundamentally change the way Black people across the country were penalized in the present, while spurring conversation about the injustices tied to cannabis from the past. Each of the subsequent legislation was using different strategies to federally change how states enforced cannabis laws, and in each effort, the legislation did not leave the House chamber. Congresswoman Lee couldn't even get the House to pass the RESPECT resolution, which acknowledged the disproportionate treatment inside of the cannabis industry. The resolution addressed social justice-related reforms that would level the playing field in the cannabis industry. After a career that has lasted close to three decades, Congresswoman Lee was still unable to get her fellow legislators to simply acknowledge the inequities in cannabis, which are primarily practiced on Black people.

Although unsuccessful with reform in the realm of cannabis, Congresswoman Lee was able to get much needed assistance to those in the Caribbean after Hurricane Dennis. On July 7, 2005, a category 4 hurricane ravaged parts of the Caribbean and continued on through Mobile, AL (National Weather Service, 2022). By the time the hurricane reached the United States, it had weakened, but not before 1,000 people had to be evacuated to temporary shelter in Haiti. Congresswoman Lee's legislative icon Shirley Chisolm along with Mervyn Dymally had created a task force around the issue of Haiti in the early 1980s. The Caucus' focus on Haiti deepen in the mid-1990s with governmental instability (Nelson, 2022). Therefore, H.R. 1409 in the 109th Congress was in-step with the legislative agenda of the CBC.

The Assistance for Orphans and Other Vulnerable Children in Developing Countries Act of 2005 amended current law. As discussed previously, women of the CBC understood the difficulty in passing legislation. Subsequently, they amended other legislation or provided resolutions to address issues that were of importance to them. In the case of Assistance for Orphans, the legislation amended the Foreign Assistance Act of 1961. The legislation authorized:

> the President to provide assistance, including through nongovernmental or international organizations, for basic care for orphans and other vulnerable children in developing countries, including assistance for: (1) community-based care; (2) school food programs; (3) education and employment training; (4) psychosocial support; (5) protection of inheritance rights; and (6) HIV/AIDS care. H.R. 1409, 109th Cong. (1st Sess. 2005)

The original legislation allowed the president to control this assistance without the specific authorization of Congress. This amendment expanded the areas in which those resources could be funded. The CBC's appeal to the moral conscious of the president was not a new strategy. In fact, members of the CBC did this quite frequently in the Newt Gingrich era because it allowed them the opportunity to connect with a sole decision maker. Although this piece of legislation passed after Gingrich was no longer speaker, this legislation gave the Bush Administration a mechanism to help those in Haiti, especially after the debacle that was Hurricane Katrina.

After the Newt Gingrich era, the country was facing a host of uncertainty. There was Y2K: uncertainty about the formatting and storage of calendar data for computers related to dates in and after the year 2000. There was the proliferation of the search engines on the internet which produced AOL, Yahoo, and Google, giving ordinary citizens access to information that was once controlled. The expansion of the digital space created more places for the American people to be taken advantage. This subsequently meant that Black Americans were more vulnerable to the shift and needed legislators who were keen to the changing faces of racism. The largest event causing a cultural shift in America was 9/11, the attack of the World Trade Center, which produced the War on Terror. During this era between 1999 and 2008, nine women became members of the CBC, but they struggled with getting legislation passed.

Stephanie Tubbs Jones was the first Black woman elected to the House of Representatives serving Ohio's 11th district. At the turn of the century, Black women were still making history by being the first. Congresswoman Jones was not finished making history; during her tenure, she was the only woman to serve as prosecutor in any major American city. Serving in both roles, she was able to see the fight of Blacks in the Cleveland area from two distinct lenses: the judiciary and the legislative. It is because of the exposure gained she consistently used legislative activism and sponsored H.R. 4328 Community Economic Development Expertise Enhancement Act. The legislation would authorize the Secretary of Housing and Urban Development to make grants to increase the capacity and expertise of community-based economic development organizations. She again chose legislative activism in her sponsorship of H.R. 1381 Count Every Vote Act, which would amend the Help America Vote Act of 2002 by:

requiring for voter verification and manual audit capacity; allow for voting systems for language minorities; prohibit undisclosed software, and wireless communication devices in voting systems and certifying all software and hardware used in electronic voting systems; establish thresholds for mandatory recounts; enhance accessibility and voter verification for disabled voters; remedial plans for States with excessive voter wait times; public reports on Federal elections; standards for purging voters; election day registration and early voting; voting rights of individuals convicted of criminal offenses; and election day as a public holiday.

As a prosecutor, she was well aware of those who had lost their right to vote due to criminal offense. As a legislator during the dawn of electronic processes, she foresaw the danger of electronic voting systems. As a Black woman, she was concerned with the inequities of others because of her own intersecting oppression. Subsequently, the sponsorship of such a comprehensive bill provided a federal roadmap for the changing nature of elections in America.

Her care for those inside of the larger Black community was evident when she sponsored H.R. 3769 Katrina Act of 2005. She was over 1,000 miles away from the affected area, still she sponsored a bill to make several changes to the low-income housing tax credit; her proposal would provide more affordable housing units expeditiously to areas devastated by Hurricane Katrina. Yet, a less comprehensive bill H.R. 3768 Katrina Emergency Tax Relief Act of 2005 was signed into law, which adjusted the tax provisions for those affected by the historic storm. Jones' bill, which was concerned with the least of these, died in committee while the adjusted tax provision bill became law in just 9 days. Congresswoman Jones stands at the doorway between the Gingrich and Y2K era. In her 9 years of service, only one piece of legislation she sponsored passed before her untimely death on August 20, 2008. Jones died of a brain aneurism, a bulge in a blood vessel caused by a weakness in the blood vessel wall. There is no evidence that her serving in both roles as prosecutor and legislator caused her death. Yet, actively fighting oppression takes a toll on your body, which is evident in the life of Congresswoman Barbara Jordan and Congresswoman Jones.

After the scare of Y2K, the CBC added seven more women to their ranks and welcomed the return of Cynthia McKinney from Georgia. Those additions included Diane Watson of California's 32nd and 33rd districts, Denise Majette of Georgia's 4th district, Gwen Moore of Wisconsin's 4th district, Laura Richardson of California's 37th district, Yvette Clarke of New York's 9th district, Donna Edwards of Maryland's 4th district, and Marcia Fudge of Ohio's 11th district.

Diane Watson of California's 32nd, latter its 33rd district, ran inside of the Democrat primary after the death of Julian Dixon. She like Barbara Lee was a woman in California taking seats that had been vacated by men. In 1978, Watson became the first Black woman to be elected to the California State Senate and was a contemporary of Lee's serving for a brief time with her in the state Senate. Watson did not marvel at being the first, but instead was committed to be visible for the communities she came to serve. While in the state Senate, she played a major role in formulating the state of California's Temporary Assistance for Needy Families (TANF) program, and continuously advocated for the law to represent those often voiceless in their legislatures.

Therefore, when Watson, a trained school psychologist, became a member of the House of Representatives joining the CBC, she was a vocal leader on racism, xenophobia, and reform of the educational system. Congresswoman Watson like Congresswoman Eddie Bernice Johnson had a formidable career before entering politics. She worked inside of the world of education using her background in psychology for the California State University system and then with the Bureau of Industrial Education in the state. She became the first Black woman to serve on the Los Angeles Unified School District Board of Education in 1975 and went on to get a PhD in education administration from Claremont Graduate School in 1987. Consequently, it is not surprising that Watson sponsored legislation that was directly connected to the inequities in educational systems.

Congresswoman Watson sponsored H.R. 1184 At-Risk Youth Protection Act of 2007 and H.R. 2554 After Care Act of 2007 in the 1st session of the 110th Congress. The At-Risk Youth Protection Act:

> Authorizes the Secretary of Education to make grants to states for subgrants to alternative public schools or programs, which serve the needs of students at risk of educational failure. Requires subgrantees to require their secondary school students to perform at least 100 hours of community service each school year and receive training or counseling on conflict

resolution as a prerequisite to performing such service. It also Amends the Internal Revenue Code to provide a tax deduction to a business of: (1) $750 per 100 hours of community service provided by such a student through such business during the taxable year; and (2) $2,000 for each graduate of such alternative school or program who completes one year of employment with such business.

The crafting of this bill directly correlates with the argument of Dowe forwarded in *Radical Imagination of Black Women.* Watson's lived experiences in education at the local level and the state level in California made her keenly aware of the challenges in education. She also understood that students who did not succeed in the classroom were more likely to be casualties of the justice system. Therefore, this legislation provides latitude to the Secretary of Education to use funds already allocated by Congress to help address the issue. The legislation is clever to connect the community to the funding while providing business incentive with a tax deduction. This speaks to Dr. Watson's understanding of intrinsic motivation. The financial resources that she sought to allocate are finite, but the ties built in the community through hours of dedicated service could have permanent consequences for the community. Yet, the bill was unsuccessful never making it to the House Floor for a vote.

Gwen Moore of Wisconsin's 4th district like Congresswoman Watson introduced legislation in the 110th Congress that would strengthen education, yet that legislation had a similar fate and died in committee. Congresswoman Moore's political trajectory was similar to many of the other Black female CBC members. She served in her state legislature in Wisconsin and was the first Black woman to serve in the state Senate; subsequently, she was the first Black woman to represent Wisconsin in the House of Representatives in 2005. She has been vocal about injustice and gained national attention as a member on the House Ways and Means Committee in the 118th Congress. She is noted for taking Brett Favre to task about funds received which were diverted from a TANF program in Mississippi (C-SPAN, 2024).

Therefore, it is not surprising that Congresswoman Moore authored the H.R. 3978 Student Breakfast and Education Improvement Act of 2007 and H.R. 7221 Homeless Emergency Assistance and Rapid Transition to

Housing Act of 2008. The Student Breakfast legislation sought to amend the Elementary and Secondary Education Act of 1965. This piece of legislation was passed during the height of civil rights legislation and was clearly passed to equalize the inequities that Black children were facing in schools that were still largely segregated. The amended legislation would require the Secretary of Education to award competitive grants to states or local educational agencies to establish or enhance school breakfast programs. The use of existing legislation in this case was important as it showed the federal government's commitment to a designated population. Therefore, the extensions of subgrants to schools where at least 65% of the students are eligible for free or reduced-price school lunches were most definitely aimed at the least of these, which are often found in Black communities. The legislation was not successful with only three congressional actions taken resulting in the legislation's death in committee.

Congresswoman Moore was more successful with H.R. 7221 Homeless Emergency Assistance and Rapid Transition to Housing Act of 2008, which passed the House of Representatives but was never assigned to a committee in the Senate. In the early and mid-2000s, high-risk mortgages became available by repackaging them into pools that were sold to investors. This enabled more first-time homebuyers to obtain mortgages and homeownership rose (Duca et al., 2011). When high-risk mortgage borrowers could not make loan payments, they either sold their homes at a gain and paid off their mortgages or borrowed more against them at higher market prices, which created the subprime mortgage crisis (DiMartino & Duca, 2007). This cycle led to home foreclosures that subsequently left many people homeless. The damage was felt largely by Blacks as they lost their homes and saw long-lasting consequences to their credit scores (Mui, 2012). Therefore, Congresswoman Moore's legislation was intentional about helping those in the Black community, the legislation:

> Expands the scope of the definition of homelessness to include unaccompanied youth and homeless families with children and youth defined as homeless under other federal statutes who: (1) have experienced a long-term period without living independently in permanent housing; (2) have experienced persistent instability as measured by frequent moves over

such period; and (3) can be expected to continue in such status for an extended period of time because of chronic disabilities, chronic physical health or mental health conditions, substance addiction, histories of domestic violence or childhood abuse, the presence of a child or youth with a disability, or multiple barriers to employment.

This legislation took into account the complexities faced by those that find themselves insecure due to the lack of permanent housing. The legislation amends McKinney-Vento Homeless Assistance Act by adjusting Title I: Housing Assistance General Provisions; Title II: Emergency Solutions Grants Program; Title III: Continuum of Care Program; Title IV: Rural Housing Stability Assistance Program; and Title V: Repeals and Conforming Amendments. This comprehensive review of the needed improvements is a testament to Congresswoman Moore's commitment to actualize the legacy of the CBC and use the Caucus' growth to produce meaningful legislation.

Congresswoman Moore was not the only Black female CBC member concerned with the effects of the subprime mortgage crisis. Laura Richardson of California's 37th district who was elected a year after Moore showed concern with H.R. 7126 HOME Act. This legislation was sponsored in the second session of the 110th Congress right before the election of Barack Obama and the saliency of the CBC in the 111th Congress. The legislation provided a clear path, which allowed those affected by the mortgage crisis to keep their home by filing:

a specified notice of default before foreclosure; and (2) make direct contact with, or exercise due diligence to contact, the borrower to provide foreclosure avoidance options. Prescribes loan modification and workout plan duties for loan servicers. Requires a covered residential mortgage agreement to grant the borrower and the mortgagee the right to negotiate a loan modification or workout plan if: (1) the mortgage is in payment default or payment default is reasonably foreseeable; or (2) the mortgagee's anticipated recovery under a loan workout plan exceeds the anticipated recovery through foreclosure on a net present value basis. Prohibits the mortgagee from refusing partial mortgage payments. Requires the mortgagee to credit such partial payments to the borrower's account. States that mortgagee acceptance of partial payments does not affect determination of mortgage default.

The legislation's aim was clear: keeping as many people in their homes as possible. Scholars argue about the cause of the crisis: Some believe that deregulation in banking prompted the crisis, while other scholars contend that market forces produced the crisis (Bernanke, 2013; Mahoney, 2018). Yet, the legislation goes further by protecting the rights of renters in a property foreclosure by:

> including a tenant(s) right to occupy the property under a lease entered into prior to foreclosure. Requires a mortgagee, where a judicial or non-judicial foreclosure has been initiated, to file a notice of sale in a public filing or recordation office before the foreclosure sale.

Congresswoman Richardson of the 37th district was in Southern California, an area of the country where the median home sales price was $415,000 in January 2008 (Hong, 2009). Richardson understood what this legislation would do for those in her district, but more importantly, she understood how this legislation would affect Black people across the nation. Although the cause of the crisis is debatable, what is clear is the lack of legislative appetite for this bill as it did not make it to the House Floor.

Yvette Clarke, a woman of Caribbean heritage, represented New York's 11th district, the same district of Shirley Chisolm. Due to redistricting, Congresswoman Clarke currently serves New York's 9th district. She is unique when comparing her to other women of the CBC. She spent a summer interning for Congressman Major Owens in his Washington, DC, office and went on to serve the same district. She cut her teeth in politics in New York's City Council in 2001. She made history succeeding her mother, former city council member Una S. T. Clarke, who held the seat for more than a decade. They were the first mother-to-daughter succession in city council (Ramirez, 2018). This succession speaks to the high visibility of Black women in their communities and the moral posture they take as legislators. The Black community of Flatbush trusted mother and daughter Clarke to continually fight for the issues that matter to them most. Congresswoman Clarke carried that fight to the House of Representatives in 2007 and it can be seen in her sponsorship of H.R. 7087 in the 110th Congress.

H.R. 7087 sought to amend the Small Business Act to establish a mentorship program. The program was designed to help minority and women-owned small businesses build their capacities and access to contracting opportunities in the construction industry. As a leader in the Bronx Overall Economic Development Corporation, Clarke saw inequities that in many cases were due to lack of mentorship. As the director of the development corporation, she understood the required infrastructure needed to be successful in business. Yet, this legislation was too prescriptive as it targeted groups with whom the larger legislature were not concerned. Yet, the saliency gained by the CBC in the 111th Congress after the election of Barack Obama helped Clarke see legislative success in the House.

In the 117th Congress, Congresswoman Clarke cosponsored landmark legislation that moved the conversation about immigration forward and passed the House of Representatives. As a second generation Jamaican American, Clarke understood that the immigration of minor children was outside of the control of the child. She also understood that the issue of immigration was often framed as an issue in the Latin community. Yet, many in the Black community, whether Caribbean or African, were also affected by the United States' broken immigration system. H.R. 6 Dream and Promise Act would give 2.5 million DREAMers temporary protected status, and deferred enforcement providing a clear pathway to citizenship. The legislation would allow the Department of Homeland Security or the Department of Justice to provide conditional permanent resident status for 10 years to a qualifying person who entered the United States. The bill imposed various qualifying requirements, such as them being continuously physically present in the United States since January 1, 2021, passing a background check, and being enrolled in or having completed certain educational programs. Unfortunately, the bill died in the Senate Judiciary committee and a different version was sponsored by Republican Sylvia R. Garcia of Texas' 29th district. The passage of this bill inside of the 117th Congress shows two things: women of the CBC have always had their sights on the prevalent issues of America, yet they are rarely given attribution for their early adoption and advocacy.

Marcia Fudge of Ohio's 11th district closes an era as the successor of the woman who opened the era: Stephanie Tubbs Jones. After her untimely death, a committee of local Democratic leaders selected Fudge as her replacement on the November ballot. This did not appear to be unusual as Fudge was the first female and first Black mayor of Warrensville Heights, OH, from 2000 to November 2008. A historical review of Fudge's Office of the Mayor page makes quite apparent her commitment to the Black community where it states:

> Mayor Fudge gathers strength from her church, The Glenville Church of God. She has modeled her life after her mother, Marian Saffold, and practices the principles of the sorority she currently serves as Immediate Past National President, Delta Sigma Theta Sorority, Inc. "You should defend those who cannot help themselves. You speak for the poor and needy and see that they get justice." Proverbs 31: 8–9. (Fudge, 2004)

She took this commitment to the House of Representative sponsoring 116 bills getting agreement on seven House Resolutions. The most important of those resolutions being H.R. 1281 and H.Con.Res. 105.

The 111th Congress H.R. 1281 celebrated the life and achievements of Dr. Dorothy Irene Height. Her life-long dedication and leadership in the struggle for human rights and equality for all people were known in the Black community. Yet, Dr. Height was invisible to most in the legislature. In 1957, she became the fourth President of the National Council of Negro Women (NCNW) and focused on ending lynching and restructuring the criminal justice system. She became a prominent voice in the Civil Rights Movement and was regularly consulted by Eleanor Roosevelt, Dwight D. Eisenhower, and Lyndon B. Johnson on political issues. Dr. Height died on April 20, 2010, and the recognition of her impact did not come by seasoned Black members of the legislature, but by the newest Black female CBC member. Congresswoman Fudge was vigilant yet again with the death of John Lewis in the 116th Congress passing H.Con.Res. 105—permitting the remains of the Honorable John Lewis, the late representative from the State of Georgia, to lie in state in the rotunda of the Capitol.

Congresswoman Fudge was elected during the height of the mortgage crisis, and her focus on defending those who could not defend themselves was clear in the legislation she sponsored. In the 111th Congress, she sponsored H.R. 2108 Predatory Mortgage Lending Practices Reduction

Act; H.R. 2794 Promoting Mortgage Responsibility Act; and H.R. 4635 Foreclosure Mandatory Mediation Act of 2010; none of this legislation made it to the House Floor. Yet, Congresswoman Fudge saw some legislative success with H.R. 2136 the Honorable Stephanie Tubbs Jones College Fire Prevention Act. In honor of her predecessor, Fudge wrote legislation that directed the Secretary of Education to make competitive grants to institutions of higher education, fraternities, and sororities to subsidize the cost of installing fire sprinkler systems, and the installation of fire suppression systems in student housing and dormitories. This legislation passed in the House but died in the Senate Committee on Health, Education, Labor, and Pensions.

President Biden and his transition team announced plans to nominate Congresswoman Fudge for Secretary of Housing and Urban Development. She appeared before the Senate Committee on Banking, Housing, and Urban Affairs on January 28, 2021 (Jan, 2021). On February 4, committee chairman Sherrod Brown advanced her nomination after a 17–7 vote in favor. On March 10, 2021, Fudge was confirmed by the Senate 66 to 34, garnering the support of every senator caucusing with the Democratic Party and 16 senators from the Republican caucus (Ryan, 2024). The first Black female mayor of Warrensville Heights, OH, was sworn in by the first Black female to become the Vice President of the United States, Kamala Harris, hours after her confirmation.

The women who served from 1995 to 2008 expanded the possibilities. Because many of them were the first of their kind, they were bold in their expression of protecting Blacks in their communities. They sponsored bold legislation that required the legislative body to grapple with issues instead of ignoring them. These women learned from their predecessors and formed solidarity requiring their colleagues in the legislative body to see them and thus the communities they were committed to serve. Some have become the road map of regrets, mistakes made, and beautiful successes to a younger generation of Black female legislators. Others have joined the ancestors, while many have retired and have provided advice from the sidelines. Expanding the collective required a tolerance for different methods and different issue foci, but it never quenched these women's commitment to the least of these.

# CHAPTER 5

## *The Resistance*

The women discussed in previous chapters allowed for the consistent resistance from these new Black women of the CBC. The women of previous generations had been the first Black female legislators; they had entered a chamber that was hostile to them; and they even had to contend with the strong male voices in the Black Caucus (Nelson, 2022). Yet, this next generation entered the chamber during a shift that their presence helped to create. From 2011 to 2023, 21 Black women were added to the CBC. Three of those women entered after the midterm election of 2010, which was squarely inside of Obama's first presidential term. Those women were Karen Bass of California's 33rd district and later 37th district, Terri Sewell of Alabama's 7th district, and Frederica Wilson of Florida's 17th district.

These women were elected while the CBC carved out chair-ships of standing committees and cemented themselves in the Democratic Party structure. All while Republicans secured a judicial win with *Citizens United v. Federal Election Commission*, they used reapportionment, which followed the 2010 census, to redistrict maps in their favor and secured 63 seats, more than the swing in the Newt Gingrich era, which resulted in John Boehner becoming Speaker of the House. The influx of money strengthened the influence of corporations in politics as the Supreme Court decision made companies people. The evidence is astounding: between 2010 and 2020, the 10 largest donors and their spouses spent a total of $1.2 billion on federal elections (Evers-Hillstrom, 2020). These competing narratives shape the ways these women have interacted inside of the legislature.

Karen Bass like many of the other female members of the CBC served in her state legislature. In fact, the year Barack Obama was elected making U.S. history, Bass made her own becoming the first Black woman to serve as a speaker of a state legislative body in California. It took the most liberal state in the union over 150 years to see a Black woman at the head of the state's legislative structure. Her ability to lead was evident; therefore, it is not surprising that the members of the CBC voted her chairwoman from 2019 to 2022 (Nelson, 2022).

Congresswoman Bass has sponsored numerous bills that speak of her commitment to the continent, to the poor, and to those in gravest need. In regard to Blacks on the continent of Africa, Bass sponsored H.R. 6472 in the 115th Congress. The Zimbabwe Democracy and Economic Recovery Amendment Act of 2018 amends the Zimbabwe Democracy and Economic Recovery Act of 2001. It establishes additional pre- and postelection conditions that Zimbabwe must satisfy in order to remove Department of the Treasury in opposition to (a) international financial institution loan, credit, or guarantee extensions to Zimbabwe or (b) cancellation of or reduction in debt owed by Zimbabwe to the United States or any international financial institution. This legislation was proposed to correct a relationship with an African country whose inflation had rose due to insurmountable debt. This legislation would have provided this African nation a much needed financial lifeline but died in committee.

Concerning the poor and those in great need, Congresswoman Bass sponsored H.R. 4998 Health Insurance for Former Foster Youth Act in the 115th Congress. The bill would require state Medicaid programs to expand coverage for former foster care youth. Specifically, state Medicaid programs would be required to cover individuals who were in foster care at 14, but subsequently left foster care due to a kinship guardianship. This legislation met a similar fate and died in committee. In the 117th Congress, she sponsored H.R. 8637 Law Enforcement De-Escalation Training Act of 2022. She sponsored this legislation after getting H.R. 1280 George Floyd Justice in Policing Act of 2021 passed in the House of Representatives days after his murder. Congresswoman Bass showed great political skill galvanizing members of the CBC and the leadership of the Democratic Party around the issue. Therefore, H.R. 8637, which would amend the Omnibus Crime Control and Safe Streets Act of 1968, was a consolation. The bill provided training on alternatives to the use of force, training on de-escalation, and trainings on mental, behavioral health, and suicidal crises.

Similar to the George Floyd Justice in Policing Act, the Law Enforcement De-Escalation Training Act went to the Senate where a separate bill was authored. The language in the Floyd Act was too strong as it removed immunity from police officers. Therefore, the bill passed by the House was not engaged; instead, Tim Scott, a Black Senator who is not a member of the CBC sponsored S.3985—JUSTICE Act. The legislation considerably watered down the language in the Floyd policing Act; yet, the JUSTICE Act was never brought to the Senate floor for a vote. John Cornyn, a senior Republican Senator from Texas, authored his own Law Enforcement De-Escalation Training Act; it watered down the language in Congresswoman Bass' bill but became law on December 27, 2022.

A year prior, Congresswoman Bass announced her run for mayor of Los Angeles. The legislative process at the federal level was not allowing her to have the impact she desired. This is evident in a statement she made in her announcement to run for mayor:

> Our city is facing a public health, safety and economic crisis in homelessness that has evolved into a humanitarian emergency ... I've spent my entire life bringing groups of people together in coalitions to solve complex problems and produce concrete change—especially in times of crisis. (White, 2021)

Bass collected a diverse group of people together to deal with the issue of police brutality and was unsuccessful in time of crisis. Therefore, the opportunity to become a member of the executive branch as mayor of Los Angeles was something that aligned with her desire and proven ability to galvanize people. In November 2022, Bass made history again becoming the first female mayor and first Black female to become mayor of Los Angeles. A *New York Times* article focused on her gender primarily (Hubler, 2022). The headline of this article shows that society is constantly asking Black women to grapple with their intersecting oppression. Often time, the society is asking Black women, like Congresswomen Bass, to place oppression in a hierarchy, which is impossible based upon the inability to isolate from either identity.

As discussed several times in this work, the Black women who became U.S. legislators have radical imaginations. They are aware that they represent those who can't defend themselves; they represent the Black people in their districts and those across the diaspora. They have been the first or watched their mentors, aunties, and mothers be the first. This was the reality for Terri Sewell of Alabama's 7th district. Congresswoman Sewell watched her mother become the first Black woman to be elected to Selma's City Council. This is undeniably powerful for those who know history. Selma is the place of Bloody Sunday, which consisted of a brutal beating during the first march for voting rights. Sewell's mother was the physical endorsement of change.

The impact of Sewell's mother, Nancy Gardner Sewell, is evident in her biographical information on her legislative district website. The Congresswoman's biography shows her commitment to civil rights, which is rooted in the example of her mother. The legislation she has sponsored and gotten passed also solidifies her commitment to those who have fought to extend democracy to all.

In the 113th Congress, she sponsored H.R. 360 and used the presidency, of the first Black man, to enshrine the triumphs of Blacks in America. H.R. 360 awarded posthumously a Congressional Gold Medal to Addie Mae Collins, Denise McNair, Carole Robertson, and Cynthia Wesley. The medal was to commemorate the lives they lost 50 years ago in the bombing of the Sixteenth Street Baptist Church in Birmingham, AL; the Church is inside of the Congresswoman's district. The aforenoted names of the four little Black girls made the ultimate sacrifice for the cause of civil rights, which demanded a movement. She understood that this symbolic act would require America to contend with who she has always been.

Congresswoman Sewell's desire to enshrine the struggle of Black humanity in American history had her to sponsor H.R. 431 in 114th Congress. This congressional session aligned with Obama's second term as president. The Act would award a Congressional Gold Medal to the Foot

Soldiers who participated in Bloody Sunday, Turnaround Tuesday, or the final Selma to Montgomery Voting Rights March in March 1965. The sponsorship of this bill confirms Sewell's understanding that her legislative career is tied to these movements. That the Voting Rights Act of 1965 allowed for the proliferation of Black legislators especially in southern states like Alabama.

Congresswoman Sewell's sponsorship of H.R. 991 in the 116th Congress displays her commitment to those in the diaspora. H.R. 991: Extension of the Caribbean Basin Economic Recovery Act allowed for the easing of tariffs due to Hurricane Dorian. This bill extended preferential duty treatment for certain apparel items produced in the Caribbean. This Act became law, which was a much needed relief for Caribbean economies affected by the lack of tourism. The Congresswoman's keen understanding of the ways to use legislation created an impact for a particular sect of Black people.

Congresswoman Sewell's ability to use symbolic legislation to have substantive impact was plausible because of a great education. Dowe (2024) noted that the Black women who hold political office are highly educated. This aligns with Sewell's educational background as the first Black valedictorian at Selma High School, after school integration. She was also the first graduate of the high school to attend Ivy League Universities; she is a contemporary of Barack Obama as they were both at Harvard Law.

Frederica Wilson of Florida's 24th district was elected during Obama's first term. She, like many other Black CBC legislators, served in Florida's state legislature. She is a graduate of Fisk University, a Historically Black University in Nashville, TN. Wilson served in both Florida's House and Senate; she rose to the party leadership position of Minority Whip. Since being elected, she has been able to steer resources to her minority–majority district. Seventy-seven million earmarked for her district to the Town of Bay Harbor Islands, FL, for "Broad Causeway Bridge Replacement" and to Neighborhood Resilience in Miami.

She has sponsored two pieces of legislation in the 116th Congress of note: H.R. 1636, which did not become law and H.R. 6213, which was enacted into law. H.R. 1636: Commission on the Social Status of Black Men and Boys Act would have established a Commission on the Social

Status of Black Men and Boys. The U.S. Commission on Civil Rights Office would lead this effort to systematically study the conditions affecting Black men and boys. This legislation was unsuccessful yet continued to drive the narrative of equalities; this narrative is the foundational work of the CBC. The growth of the caucus has allowed for different legislative strategies not available to previous generations. The evolution of the Black Caucus and its growth has required an evolution in tactics toward the goal of equality.

Wilson's legislative success came with H.R. 6213, which was enacted into law in the 116th Congress. H.R. 6213: No Cost for COVID-19 Testing Act required private health insurance plans to cover testing for COVID-19. This legislation shifted the financial responsibility during a public health emergency, which was declared on January 31, 2020. This bill had 207 cosponsors, which is close to half of the members in the House. Congresswoman Wilson and others understood that wellness during the pandemic was cost prohibitive. Therefore, legislation that reduces the barriers increases the chances of recovery. Yet, the bill also helped those who frequently have the least access to financial resources: Black people.

Joyce Beatty of Ohio's 3rd district was elected in a special election. She served in the Ohio state legislature becoming the first female Democratic House leader in Ohio's history. She, like Congresswoman Wilson, graduated from a Black institution as an alumnus of Central State University. The Congresswoman embodies legislative activist; she was arrested at a protest in July 2021 at the Senate Hart building. The protest was over voting rights, especially the John Lewis Voting Rights Advancement Act, which is named for the late congressman and civil rights icon. Beatty was the successor to Congresswoman Bass as chairwoman of the CBC from 2021 to 2023. She is a vocal legislator who sponsors provocative legislation during the final years of the Obama presidency and in the Biden Administration.

Congresswoman Beatty sponsored H.R. 5277 in the 115th Congress, which was signed by the president, becoming law on May 24, 2018. H.R. 5277: Financial Literacy College Education Act required the Financial Literacy and Education Commission to establish and publish best practices for teaching financial literacy at the collegiate level. This affected

HBCUs through information, which assisted students when making financial decisions related to the student borrowing. Black students who are first generation in college need women like Congresswoman Beatty; she, like many other female CBC women, is thinking about protecting those who don't know they need protection.

In the 117th Congress, Congresswoman, Beatty sponsored H.R. 3891, which was signed by President Biden on March 15, 2022. H.R. 3891: Trafficking Survivors Housing Act of 2021 commissioned a study on homelessness, which focused on the most vulnerable: human trafficking victims. Specifically, the study must assess housing shortages and housing instability. The study identified best practices in meeting the housing and service needs of those individuals. This legislation provided insights that Black female mayors across the country, like Karen Bass, could articulate potential impact in municipalities. As a legislative activist, Congresswoman Beatty has pushed the structure to address inequities with H.R. 5911 (117th) 2021: Fair Hiring in Banking Act or Examining and H.R. 8142 (118th) 2023: Educational Redlining in Lending Act. She was the gateway for six other Black women who joined the CBC with the Caucus' first female Republican.

The Obama Administration closed out with the addition of six more women in the CBC from across the country. In 2013, it was Robin Kelly from Illinois 2nd district; in 2014, Alma Adams from North Carolina's 12th district and Mia Love from Utah's 4th district; in 2015, Bonnie Watson Coleman of New Jersey's 12th district, Brenda Lawrence from Michigan's 14th district, and Stacey Plaskett a nonvoting member of the Virgin Islands. This group of women was diverse geographically, ideologically, and generationally. These six women represent Generation X, Baby Boomers, and those of the Silent Generation (Dimock, 2019). Yet, their commitment to be legislators that resist the normalcy of inequity was evident; they sponsored legislation around education, protecting the homeland and caring for its Veterans, and issues surrounding COVID-19.

In the area of education, this group of CBC women sponsored three pieces of legislation in the 114th and 116th Congress. Brenda Lawrence from Michigan's 14th district sponsors H.R. 1900: National Sea Grant College Program Amendments Act. The bill requires the National

Oceanic and Atmospheric Administration to award fellowships to support graduate students in fields related to ocean, coastal, and Great Lakes. Congresswoman Lawrence entered politics through the Southfield Board of Education where she served as president, vice president, and secretary. She became Southfield, MI's, first Black female mayor and was elected to four consecutive terms. As mayor of a suburb of Detroit, she had to ensure her residents had water. Therefore, as a national legislator she had an opportunity to allocate resources to best study the availability of water. The legislation died in committee yet, the lack of legislative success has not stopped her commitment sponsoring H.R. 413 in the 115th Congress the Early Pell Promise Act, or the Pell to Grad Act in the 116th and 117th Congress.

In regard to education, Alma Adams of North Carolina's 12th district, sponsored two pieces of legislation with one enacted into law. Congresswoman Adams is an educator with a PhD in Art Education and Multicultural Education from Ohio State University. Dr. Adams was faculty at Bennett College, an HBCU in Greensboro, NC, for over 30 years. She is also a graduate of North Carolina A&T in Greensboro; therefore, it is not surprising that she sponsored H.R. 1054: HBCU PARTNERS Act. The HBCU Propelling Agency Relationships toward a New Era of Results for Students Act addresses Black institutions' capacity to participate in federal programs. In particular, the Act wanted a report produced on how agencies intended to increase the capacity of HBCUs in competition for grants, contracts, or cooperative agreements. In addition, the bill provided statutory authority for the President's Board of Advisors on HBCUs. The bill failed in committee, but this did not stop Congresswoman Adams from sponsoring another education bill later in the session.

On December 19, 2019, President Donald Trump signed H.R. 5363: the FUTURE Act into law. This bill permanently authorized funding for minority-serving institutions of higher education while increasing the authorization of appropriations for Pell Grants. HBCU campuses are dominated by students that are Pell Grant eligible. Therefore, this legislation was intended to directly affect Black students. The bill also directs the IRS to disclose tax return information to determine eligibility for the recertifying for income-contingent student loan programs, discharges of loans based on disability, and the amount of student financial aid under the Higher Education Act of 1965.

Unfortunately, Congresswoman Adams is not given attribution for this shift in HBCU finance. Instead, President Trump has used the legislation, sponsored by a Black woman, to assert what he has done for Black Americans. Yet, Congresswoman Adams' life experience informed her of a need for the community in which she represents. Therefore, the impact provided is more important because attribution would require some sense of approval. As discussed early in the work, approval is a resource that is available to those with access to rationality, which is foreign for a Black woman.

In the category of protecting the homeland and caring for its veterans, CBC women who enter the house during President Obama's second term sponsored H.R. 7747 in the 116th Congress and H.R. 370 in the 117th Congress. H.R. 7747 was sponsored by Robin Kelly of Illinois 2nd district. A review of her biography shows her diverse educational accomplishments as well as her commitment to the health and wellness of vulnerable communities. Therefore H.R. 7747 is in alignment with her life experience; the act directed the Secretary of Veterans Affairs to submit to Congress an annual report on the Solid Start program. The Solid Start program is an outreach program for those in their first year of separation from the military. Research done by Syracuse University Institute for Veterans and Military Families found that 55% of Black veterans characterized their financial transition as difficult or very difficult, compared with 48% of White/Non-Hispanic veteran respondents (Institute for Veterans and Military Families, 2022).

Dr. Kelly's degrees in psychology and counseling helped inform this legislation. As an advocate of wellness, her education informs her that stress is a large component . The research done at Syracuse reveals racial tension in Black soldiers' transition into civilian life. Therefore, legislation that requires reports about Veterans transitions appears to be the legislative branch monitoring the executive. Although this legislation did not become law, it illuminated a strategy used by women of the CBC after reaching saliency in the 111th Congress. Women of the CBC have passed House Resolutions for impact and purposed amendments to established legislation. Yet, legislation that incites commissions, produces reports, and spur studies provides the foundation for evidence of historic and persistent inequities. That strategy is used in the 117th Congress with H.R. 370, which passed the House of Representatives but stalled in the Senate.

Bonnie Watson Coleman of New Jersey's 12th district is the first Black woman to represent New Jersey in the House of Representatives. She was the cofounder of the Congressional Caucus on Black Women and Girls, founded on March 29, 2016. Their mission is to advance issues and legislation important to the welfare of women and girls of African descent. This formalizes a long-held commitment of CBC women to advocate for these vulnerable groups. Their use of governmental reports is often used to expose the experiences of vulnerable groups. H.R. 370: Quadrennial Homeland Security Review Technical Corrections Act makes numerous changes to the quadrennial homeland security reviews. Specifically, the changes are related to consultation, prioritization, resources required, deadlines, and documentation. Demanding oversight through legislation creates the ability to track resources. The tracking of resources over time allows for data to tell the story of inequity. Although newer generations of CBC women have used long-term resistance plans, they still sponsored legislation that dealt with the immediate needs of their constituents created by COVID-19.

Congresswoman Alma Adams from North Carolina's 12th district sponsored H.R. 6801: FEED the Children Act in the 116th Congress. Robin Kelly from Illinois 2nd district sponsored H.R. 6244; each of these pieces of legislation died in House committees. Adams' FEED the Children Act directed the Department of Agriculture (USDA) to allocate additional funds to states to partially reimburse school food programs from March 2020 through June 2020. This was during the height of uncertainties caused by the COVID-19 pandemic. Congresswoman Kelly sponsors H.R. 6244: To amend titles XVIII and XIX to provide for coverage at no-cost sharing of COVID-19 testing under the Medicaid program and Children's Health Insurance Program. These pieces of legislation show that the women of the CBC can work on long-term resistance strategies, while pushing legislators in the House to address specific issues that plague Black communities. The next set of CBC women are elected during Donald Trump's presidency.

The 2016 election was historic because, for the first time in American history, a woman was the candidate for a major party: the Democratic

Party. Hillary Clinton, a former First Lady, Senator from New York, and Secretary of State in the Obama Administration, does not win the election. Instead, Donald Trump who had never held a government position became the 45th president of the United States. The progress seen in the Obama Administration and the threat of regression saw a host of Black women elected from 2017 to 2019: Lisa Blunt Rochester of Delaware's At-Large district, Val Demings of Florida's 10th district, Brenda Jones of Michigan's 13th district, Jahana Hayes of Connecticut's 5th district, Lucy McBath of Georgia's 6th district, Ilhan Omar of Minnesota's 5th district, Ayanna Pressley of Massachusetts 7th district, and Lauren Underwood of Illinois' 14th district. These women were concerned about the welfare of others authoring legislation concerning the environment and healthcare. They used the expansion of the CBC to cosponsor bills and see legislative success. The Black CBC women in this group knew they were legislating in times of White backlash, which was evident with the election of Donald Trump.

Sponsoring legislation as a group had success in the 116th and 117th Congress but did not ensure all legislation would become law. This group was clear about the landscape that is American politics. This is evident in the history these Black women made. Ilhan Omar was the first Somali American in the U.S. Congress and the first woman of two Muslim women alongside Rashida Tlaib. Val Demings joined Congress after being the first female chief of the Orlando Police Department. Lucy McBath of Georgia's 6th district beat Republican opponents in both 2018 and 2020; Republicans were determined to win back the seat once held by Newt Gingrich, the arbitrator of the modern-day House of Representatives. McBath is the mother of Jordan Davis who was murdered at a Gate Petroleum gas station in Jacksonville, FL. The racially motivated shooting was perpetrated by Michael David Dunn, a White male, following an argument over loud music played by Davis and his three friends (Santiago, 2020). Jahana Hayes was the first Black woman and first Black Democrat to represent Connecticut in Congress. Lastly, Lisa Blunt Rochester of Delaware is the first woman and first Black to represent Delaware in Congress. She will go on to be the first woman and Black to represent Delaware in the U.S. Senate for the 119th Congress.

In the 116th Congress, Congresswoman McBath sponsored H.R. 2938 the HAVEN Act. The legislation had 38 cosponsors. The female CBC cosponsors are numerous, contributing to close to a third of the cosponsors. They were as follows: Lisa Blunt Rochester, Yvette Clark, Shelia Jackson Lee, Karen Bass, Gwen Moore, Del. Stacey Plaskett, Frederica Wilson, Eddie Bernice Johnson, Bonnie Watson Coleman, Marcia Fudge, and Del. Eleanor Holmes Norton. HAVEN is an acronym for Honoring American Veterans in Extreme Need, and the bill modifies the treatment of certain veterans' benefits in bankruptcy. The bill excluded from a debtor's current monthly income certain benefits, which included disability benefits paid by the Department of Veterans Affairs or the Department of Defense. This bill significantly reduced the amount of income ascribed to veterans who were filing bankruptcy. The reduction in income reduced the amount a veteran had to pay to a bankruptcy court undoubtedly affecting Black veterans.

McBath used armed conflicts and attacks in Libya on July 11 to gather 30 cosponsors for a bill introduced on May 23, 2019 (Reuters, 2019). She was adroit at ceasing the political moment to push a bill that helped veterans. She also went to the bullpen of the CBC and relied on the support of Black female legislators to get the legislation to pass the House of Representatives. Due to the political moment, the legislation was not assigned to committee in the Senate yet was passed with a Senate voice vote on August 1, 2019. The exclusion of income paid by the Department of Veterans Affairs or the Department of Defense in bankruptcy became law on August 23, 2019, because of the shrewd legislative skill of a Black woman.

The use of collectivity to advocate for and deliver legislation for those who could not advocate for themselves is also seen with the passage of H.R. 7791 in the 117th Congress. Unlike the HAVEN Act, which was not gender specific, the Access to Baby Formula Act of 2022 was directed to help poor mothers. COVID-19 created supply chain disruptions that affected most industries. This disruption was not lost on the women of the CBC; subsequently, Congresswoman Jahana Hayes sponsored a bill to address supply chain disruptions affecting participants of the Special Supplemental Nutrition Program for Women, Infants, and Children (WIC). The legislation had 129 cosponsors, which included all the women of the CBC elected after the 2016 presidential election. The bill authorized the USDA to waive or modify any WIC-qualified administrative requirement during emergencies, disasters, and supply chain disruptions. This allowed mothers to exceed the maximum monthly allowance for infant formula. In each of these cases, Black female legislators were able to use crisis to produce legislation with a collection of Black female voices. This legislative strategy was not fail-proof because it did not ensure legislative success in the Senate.

Congresswoman Lauren Underwood sponsored H.R. 958 in the 117th Congress. Protecting Moms Who Served Act of 2021 was cosponsored by several CBC who were elected after 2016, which included the following Congresswomen: Hayes, Pressley, Blunt Rochester, and McBath. The bill passed the House of Representatives but died in the Senate Committee on Veterans' Affairs. It is possible that the legislation was too prescriptive as the bill required the Department of Veterans Affairs (VA) to implement the maternity care coordination program. The program was designed to respect the unique needs of pregnant and postpartum veterans, particularly regarding mental and behavioral health conditions. In addition, the law required the Government Accountability Office to report on maternal mortality and severe maternal morbidity among pregnant and postpartum veterans focusing on racial and ethnic disparities in maternal health outcomes for veterans. These Black women had heard the horror stories of Black maternal mortality and brought legislation to study the phenomenon and collect data. Yet, the support they amassed in the House of Representatives did not translate in the Senate. Although progress had been made, the inability to get this racialized piece of legislation to the president's desk highlights the racial strife and gender disillusionment that persist in the U.S. legislature.

The obstacles up against these women did not stop them from sponsoring legislation that brought awareness to issues others in Congress would rather ignore. In the 116th Congress, Lisa Blunt Rochester sponsored H.R. 536: Safe Drinking Water Assistance Act of 2019, which addressed emerging contaminants not regulated or monitored by the Environmental Protection Agency (EPA) that may have adverse effects on human health. Or H.R. 8144 sponsored by Congresswoman Jahana Hayes in the 116th

Congress concerned with VA Mental Health Staffing. These women did not allow their status as junior legislators to stop them from sponsoring legislation around issues they were passionate about because they were clear about their role to resist.

The expansion of the CBC allowed these women to sit on a variety of committees, which allowed Black female legislators the opportunity to speak on issues that are not attributed to political Blackness. Ilhan Omar alongside Barbara Lee sat on the House Committee on the Budget in the 118th Congress. Or Lauren Underwood alongside Barbara Lee and Bonnie Watson Coleman on the House Committee on Appropriations in the 118th Congress. Committees once out of reach for Congressional Black Caucus members boost two and three CBC members. This is certainly the case of the House Committee on Agricultural who saw four women from the CBC in the 118th Congress. Jahana Hayes alongside Alma Adams welcomed Jasmine Crockett, who succeeded Eddie Bernice Johnson in Texas' 30th district, and Shontel Brown of Ohio's 11th district, who secured the seat vacated by Marcia Fudge.

This last group of female CBC members are packaged around two women Cori Bush of Missouri's 1st district and Jasmine Crockett of Texas' 30th district. They represent the final female expansion of the CBC and symbolize the spectrum of Blackness seen throughout America. The expansion of the Caucus up to this time had displayed ideological differences but have not highlighted the social and economic strata of Blacks in America. This in many ways was by design because Black people have historically needed to be seen as the chief moralist for viability in the legislature structure (Nelson, 2022).

Many CBC members from the old guard were retiring and dying. This provided the opportunity to answer a lingering question in the field of Black politics: Was the legislative ground won with the Civil Rights Act of 1965 sustainable? Would the historic gerrymandering of districts make it possible to maintain minority–majority districts across the United States? The death of John Lewis, the civil rights activist of Georgia's 6th district, answered this question. Nikema Williams whose great-aunt Autherine Lucy integrated the University of Alabama won his seat (Bash, 2021). The question about legacy minority–majority district was cemented inside of Florida's 17th district. The death of Alcee Hastings produced Shelia Cherfilus-McCormick, a Howard University graduate who won the seat becoming the only Haitian American Democrat ever elected to Congress (Joseph, 2022).

During the Biden–Harris Administration, Bush, Crockett, Williams, and Cherfilus-McCormick were not the only four Black women who joined the CBC. There were seven more women: Marilyn Strickland of Washington's 10th district, Shontel Brown of Ohio's 11th district, Valerie Foushee of North Carolina's 4th district, Sydney Kamlager-Dove of California's 37th district, Summer Lee of Pennsylvania's 12th district, Emilia Sykes of Ohio's 13th district, Jennifer McClellan of Virginia's 4th district, and LaMonica McIver of New Jersey's 10th district. These seven women were reelected and returned to the House of Representatives for the 119th Congress. Many of these women aligned with the developed formula for rising to the national legislature, by being the first of their kind. Marilyn Strickland of Washington's 10th district is an example as the first Black woman mayor of Tacoma, WA, and the first Black woman to represent the state of Washington. Or Summer Lee of Pennsylvania's 12th district who was the first Black woman to represent Pennsylvania in the House of Representatives after serving in the state legislature.

For the life of the CBC, there has long been a "type" of person who ascends to legislative heights at the national level. Dowe (2024) categorizes the women as super joiners; women who are active in multiple civic organizations with the Greek letter organizations lead the way. However, to much chagrin, respectability politics and the image of the "talented tenth" has been the order of the day. To be seen as a viable Black legislator, CBC members have desired those of their same elk and this has been of even more importance for the women of the CBC. Looking a particular way, coming from the right family, graduating from an HBCU or Ivy League school, being a member of a historically Black sorority have been lynchpins for success.

More importantly, political development at the state legislative level has been key for the rise of Black female legislators to the House of Representatives. Time spent in the state legislature results in a level of political refinement, which appears to be the unspoken rule in Black women's eligibility to run for a congressional seat. This has evolved, and political leadership as mayor, council person, or a member of the local school board has sufficed. Yet, the requirement of political refinement has remained. This is evident in the political trajectories of two CBC female peers. Both were reared in St. Louis, MO, but Cori Bush and Jasmine Crockett's ascension to the House of Representatives was quite different.

Congresswoman Crockett is not a graduate of a Historically Black College or University, but a lifetime member of Delta Sigma Theta Sorority, Inc. Prior to serving in Washington, DC, she spent a term in the Texas House of Representatives. Crockett was a practicing public defender before beginning her political career taking cases pro bono for Black Lives Matter protestors (Taylor et al., 2022). Crockett fits into the tried-and-true mold of CBC women before her. She is outspoken but performs with a political flare and rhetorical prowess that is respected and unmistakable. Congresswoman Crockett became the fodder of national attention when she used her knowledge of House protocol to "play the dozens."

Lefever (1981) in his article "'Playing the Dozens': A Mechanism for Social Control" contends that, for many years in numerous Black communities, Blacks have ritualized a verbal contest of insult. The usual setting for the game is the low-income areas of our major cities. It is also played by middle-class boys and men. The game is spurred by an insult of a person or member of another's family; others in the group make disapproving sounds to spur on the coming exchange. The retort must be clever enough to defend one's honor and reduce the likelihood of further jibes. Congresswoman Crockett used this exact mechanism when ridiculing Congresswoman Majorie Taylor Greene of Georgia's 14th district in 2024.

Crockett, in what appeared to be an attempt to clarify the limits on personal comments, was prepared to verbally spare in a House Oversight and Accountability Committee meeting in May 2024 (Kurtz, 2024). She asked "If someone on this committee then start talking about somebody's bleach-blonde, bad-built, butch body, that would not be engaging in personalities, correct?" This displayed a cunning wit that showed her mastery of legislative procedure infused with cultural sophistication.

This increased her national visibility resulting in a mirage of media opportunities from mainstream media and grassroot activist forums. Crockett's visibility has made her a well-known CBC member whose constituents wanted to see continuous fight in Congress, which is evident in decisive win of her district on November 5, 2024 (AP News, 2024).

On the contrary, Cori Bush is the picture of the exception and not the rule. She came to the House of Representative directly on the heels of founding a church, Kingdom Embassy International Church in St. Louis, MO. Bush had no real political experience prior to making her way to Congress. She was known in the community as an activist who ended the Clay family dynasty. William Lacy "Bill" Clay Sr. was a founding member of the CBC in 1971, and he was succeeded by his son William Lacy Clay, Jr., who lost to Bush in 2020 (Nelson, 2022). Bush was the leading activist in 2014 as unrest in Ferguson, MO, sprung due to the murder of Michael Brown. Upon election in 2020, Bush was almost immediately grouped together with "The Squad" making her even more the exception and not the rule.

The Squad is a progressive group of legislators who are members of the Congressional Progressive Caucus in the House of Representatives. After the 2018 midterm elections during the Trump presidency, Alexandria Ocasio-Cortez of New York, Ilhan Omar of Minnesota, Ayanna Pressley of Massachusetts, and Rashida Tlaib of Michigan established the group. Following the 2020 House of Representatives elections, newly elected Jamaal Bowman of New York and Cori Bush of Missouri joined. In the 2022 midterm elections, Greg Casar of Texas, Summer Lee of Pennsylvania, and Delia Ramirez of Illinois became members. These legislators appreciated her activist leanings, and Cori Bush continued to display them in Washington, DC, by sleeping on the steps of the U.S. Capitol. She along with Ayanna Pressley and Alexandria Ocasio-Cortez was fighting to extend the CARES Act's eviction moratorium; they were successful as the CDC extended the moratorium soon after. When asked why she participated, she stated, "I slept on the Capitol steps because I've been evicted three times in my life" (Bush, 2021).

Bush did not "look the part" either, as she was not concerned with appearing polished in her attire. Indiscriminate of fashion preferences, all the women of the CBC confirmed to the congressional norm of professional attire. Not only did Bush conform, but she did not have a signature fashion staple like a cowboy hat or impeccable colorful suits. Instead, there was the frequent sighting of a chest tattoo, which was frowned upon by Blacks in the community, while being viewed by some in the CBC as demeaning the role of Black legislators. Bush wasn't known for her rhetorical skill and was often seen as speaking too plainly, whereas Crockett's speaking style, though culturally relevant, is lauded and can be attributed to the time she spent in the courtroom and on the Texas legislative floor.

In the 2024 elections, Bowman and Bush faced Democratic challengers in their respective primaries. Bush was replaced by Wesley Bell and Bowman by George Stephen Latimer, which means both will be left the Squad in the 119th Congress. These differences between Crockett and Bush illuminate intra-racial relations. Their differences highlight the ways social strata play a role in branding, creating two district images. Crockett is seen as the poster child for the new wave of CBC women, and Bush is seen as anomaly who slipped through the cracks. Bush was very concerned with fighting for her constituents , as is Crockett, but Bush was unconcerned with meeting some of the political criteria, which marks a lengthy tenure in Congress, especially for women. Cori Bush's vote against President Biden's Infrastructure Investment and Jobs Act spelled her demise. It showed her unwillingness to vote with the Democratic Party and underscored her unwillingness to glad-hand with the right congressional powerholders. Seven of the eleven women elected during the Biden Administration attended HBCUs. Their attendance provided these women with established Black networks; networks filled with educated Black people who had access to social strata not readily available to Cori Bush.

The slot of junior female CBC legislators elected from 2020 were committed to resistance but not tied to activist methodologies. Many of these women were not new to politics and had a political sophistication that had been tested before their ascension to the national stage. Therefore, there was a lack of timidity in sponsoring legislation. This is seen in the 117th Congress, when Marilyn Strickland, a junior legislator, sponsored H.R. 5470: HOMES for our Veterans Act of 2021.

The legislation amended title 38 of the U.S. Code to improve grants awarded by the Secretary of Veterans Affairs to serve homeless veterans. Strickland as a former mayor of a major city understood how local municipalities struggle with providing shelter for those unhoused. In 2022, VA reported 33,129 veterans were homeless (Diaz, 2023). Strickland used her former political experiences to quickly address the national issue in a prescribed incremental way. Her focus on veterans allowed for data to tell a compelling story about those who once defended freedom. Her political life experiences attribute to this legislation becoming law on December 29, 2022.

Junior female CBC women saw legislative success again in the 117th Congress with the passage of H.R. 5577. Nikema Williams sponsored the legislation that designated the facility at 3900 Crown Road Southwest in Atlanta, GA, as the "John R. Lewis Post Office Building." All the CBC members cosponsored the bill. It was fitting that Williams, Lewis' successor, a graduate of Talladega College, which is historically connected to the civil rights movement, was the author (Talladega College, n.d.). Legislative success was seen once again on account of John Lewis with H.R. 1150 in the 118th Congress.

In the 118th Congress, Congresswoman Williams alongside all the women of the CBC sponsored the John Lewis Civil Rights Fellowship Act of 2023. The bill established the John Lewis Civil Rights Fellowship Program within the J. William Fulbright Educational Exchange Program. The legislation was in alignment with the CBC women's focus on education and commitment to the equal treatment of all. The fellowship program was designed to advance U.S. foreign policy priorities by promoting studies, research, and international exchange in the subject of nonviolent civil rights movements that occurred throughout the world. This legislation went further than a symbolic building. This legislation highlights the global impact John Lewis had and thus the CBC has had on the evolution of democracy.

Yet, all the legislation sponsored by this group of women was not successful. Congresswoman Sydney Kamlager-Dove sponsored H.R. 9835 in the 118th Congress. The Sexual Abuse Services in Detention Act was cosponsored by four junior CBC female legislators Summer Lee, Jasmine Crockett, Robin Kelly, and Lauren Underwood, and one veteran Del.

Eleanor Holmes Norton. The legislation authorized grants for emotional support services for incarcerated victims of sexual abuse. The emotional support services, or counseling for individuals, included the following: crisis intervention services; education about the dynamics of sexual abuse and sexual harassment; and assistance with processing traumatic experiences, while building coping skills. The legislation did not leave the House Committee on the Judiciary. It is important to note that the 118th Congress has been one of the least productive Congresses in the nation's history. Only 78 pieces of legislation had become law after the summer recess in August of 2024 (Shutt, 2024). Therefore, the success seen by these women in the final group elected to the Congressional Black Caucus speaks to the dedication of the women of the CBC to resist at all stages of the Caucus' evolution.

# CHAPTER 6
## *Black Female Senators*

In 118th Congressional sessions, there have only been 12 Black people in the U.S. Congress: Hiram R. Revels and Blanche K. Bruce of Mississippi; Tim Scott of South Carolina and Raphael G. Warnock of Georgia; Cory A. Booker of New Jersey; Edward W. Brooke III and William Cowan of Massachusetts; Kamala D. Harris and Laphonza R. Butler of California; and Carol Moseley Braun, Barack Obama, and Roland Burris of Illinois. Johnson et al. (2012) in "The House as a Stepping Stone to the Senate: Why Do So Few African American House Members Run?" presents contextual factors linked to race, such as state population, ability to raise campaign funds, and ideological extremity, which play a role in the strategic decision to run (Johnson et al., 2012). State racial population is a sound augment for Hiram R. Revels and Blanche K. Bruce of Mississippi who were Senators during the reconstruction era. The ability to raise campaign funds is a sound argument for Georgia Senator Raphael Warnock. He raised more money than any other candidate in the 2022 midterms at $176 million by December 2022 (USAFacts, 2023). These variables create particular barriers that many Blacks just cannot overcome.

Historically, the U.S. Senate has been the gateway to the American presidency. There have been 46 terms for the presidency, which have been filled by 32 men. Only 14 men have had more than one term with Franklin Delano Roosevelt having three (White House History, 2024). Of those 32 men, 17 have been U.S. Senators starting with James Monroe in 1817 to 1825 and ending with Joseph R. Biden who served from 2021 to 2025 (U.S. Senate, 2024). Becoming a Senator for a state shows the ability to substantially raise funds and bridge ideological extremity across a diverse set of people. As a senator you are not concerned with a district of roughly 700,000 people. Instead, you must represent the interest of millions of people who, depending on the closeness of the race, may not have voted for you. It is the first time in representational democracy that you may represent people that do not ideologically agree with you. This mimics itself at the presidential level where the electoral college elects the president and not the popular vote. Therefore, senators like presidents have to represent all those in a designated territory requiring trust in a person's decision making.

Smith (2010) in "Race and Trust" articulates that race is the most important determinant of trust. The article continues to argue that the trust gap is starkest between Blacks and Whites but cannot easily be accounted for by traditional factors like class. Instead, historical and contemporary discrimination provides the largest explanation. Therefore, this gap in trust woven into the selection of a U.S. Senator is best closed by White men. Ethno-racial socialization and neighborhood context explain ethno-racial differences in generalized trust. Simply put, the lack of racial diversity in one's community embeds a structure of distrust of those who do not look like you. Therefore Blacks, indiscriminate of gender, struggle to gain strategic trust from those outside of their racial group.

The ability to trust is linked to rationality of decisions made. As stated earlier, full rationality is reserved for White men. They have access to rational resources, time, information, approval, and prestige. The use of these resources justifies and rationalizes their choices, which results in a holistic trust of White men that is not often challenged. This allows for an inherent masculinity in decision making that is not available to women and most certainly not available to Black women. Han and Heldman in *Madam President: Gender and Politics on the Road to the White House* discuss the office of the presidency, prevalent negative stereotypes of women leaders, gender bias in news coverage of woman politicians, and a lack of potential women candidates due to so few women holding political positions (Beail et al., 2022). An examination of these factors revels the masculine nature of the American presidency, which is linked to the U.S. Senate.

Masculine conceptions of presidential leaders are embedded in American society through the media. In *Madam President*, the authors find that voters prefer more masculine candidates for the presidency, so candidates engage in feminization of their opponents. Men are consistently discussed as tough and aggressive by the media, which reinforces that leadership is masculine, and presidential leadership especially so. This is why the feminization of other male opponents is important to indirectly drive the idea that women are not to be trusted with such a leadership role. Sports metaphors in relationship with presidential politics is another signal to masculinity. The use of game or contests serves to symbolically exclude women candidates. Stereotypes of women as cautious and soft-spoken are in opposition to ideation of sports or gaming culture. It is not societally acceptable for a woman to crush an opponent as typically done in sports, which is associated with manhood.

The hurdle of masculinity was engaged by Senator Hillary Clinton; a woman who only had to contend with sexism not the intersection of race and gender. A review of the 2016 election, where sexual misconduct was attached to each candidate, shows how the nation handled each candidate differently. Heldman et al. (2018) asserts that masculinity and sexism effected how the nation handled Trump's multiple allegations of sexual violence. Trump used these allegations to bolster his manhood, which speaks directly of the masculine requirements of the presidency. In contrast, Hillary Clinton's handling of her husband's alleged sexual assaults disqualified her for the presidency. This assertion is cemented by Trump's bragging about sexual assault in the Access Hollywood tape and winning the presidency by weaponizing the allegations of sexual misconduct. Trump's ability to win the White House in 2016 speaks of the robust conflation of the presidency and masculinity.

Heldman also contends that the prototypical citizenship limit identifies who can "legitimately" hold the office of presidency. This is seen in the election of Senator Barack Obama whose American citizenship was challenged during his presidency (Gore, 2017). A majority of Americans think of the prototypical citizen is White and male. The American presidency is symbolic for the ideal citizen; therefore, women and Blacks don't provide a symbol that can be accepted. This narrow conception of prototypical citizenships poses a challenge not only for the presidency but simultaneously in the Senate, which serves as providing ground for citizenry appeal.

This engagement with masculinity and refusal to see Blacks as citizens explains why there have only been three Black women to serve in the U.S. Senate. Black women due to their intersecting oppression have to engage the myth of White Supremacy and social norms that assign executive leadership to men. This is why Carol Moseley Braun of Illinois, and Kamala Harris and Laphonza Butler of California have been the only Black women to serve in the U.S. Senate. It is important to note that Senator Butler was appointed to the seat after it was vacated by Kamala Harris with the election of Joseph Biden as president and Harris as vice president. The 119th Congress will be historic as two Black women Angela Alsobrooks of Maryland and Lisa Blunt Rochester of Delaware will serve simultaneously, making it the first time two Black women served in the U.S. Senate.

The sheer lack of Black members in the Senate makes a racial caucus like the CBC appealing to Black members. The Caucus was founded in the House of Representatives by Black Democratic members who wanted the autonomy to speak for the needs of Black folks. The Caucus sprang out of the Democratic Select Committee, which was founded in 1969 after the gains seen by the Civil Rights Act of 1965. Many in the committee struggled with a notion of gratitude that was constantly presented by the legislative body, which stoked the need for an autonomous racial body (Nelson, 2022). Therefore, the ability to caucus around the issue of race for Black senatorial members is only possible with the inclusion inside of the CBC.

Carol Moseley Braun was the first Black woman to be elected in the Senate in 1992. She was clear about what her election meant to the nation and to the larger Black community. This sentiment is capture in a statement made shortly after she was sworn into office; she states, "I cannot escape the fact that I come to the Senate as a symbol of hope and change … Nor would I want to, because my presence in and of itself will change the U.S. Senate" (Moseley Braun, 1994). During her single term, the Senator Moseley Braun worked to address issues that many Black women before her championed: improvements in civil rights and legislation on crime, education, and families.

Senator Moseley Braun is a product of Chicago, IL, born, raised, and reared. She was born on August 16, 1947, and lived in segregated housing on Chicago's south side (Moseley Braun, 1994). She attended Parker High School, which is now Paul Robeson High School, and earned a bachelor's degree in political science from the University of Illinois in 1969. In 1972, Moseley Braun graduated from the University of Chicago School of Law; showing herself to be a leader, she founded the school Black Law Students' Association, which still exists today (Black Law Students' Association, 2022). Moseley Braun worked as a prosecutor in the office of the U.S. Attorney in Chicago from 1973 until 1977. It was during this time that she interfaced with the ills of the criminal justice system that spurred her legislative activism.

In 1978, she won election to the Illinois state House of Representatives. Like many of the CBC female women before her, she served d in the state legislature, which allowed for the development of political sophistication, especially after serving for a decade. Her time in Illinois state legislator aligned with the election of Harold Washington, the first Black mayor in Chicago. This allowed Moseley Braun an opportunity to work with this powerful mayoral administration that changed the lives of Black people in Chicago. In a quest to have more direct impact, she ran for lieutenant governor of Illinois in 1986 but was not successful. Yet in 1988, Moseley Braun became the Black to hold an executive position in Cook County (Nordgren, 1992).

A historical event that conflated her identities as Black and female led to her historic run for the U.S. Senate. A review of her biography, and confirmation provided by a recorded interview, reveals Moseley Braun's motivation to make history: Supreme Court nominee Clarence Thomas. She explains how she watched the controversial confirmation hearing and how several Senators dismissively questioned Anita Hill. This was a watershed moment as the testimony of a Black woman was being ignored by those who had the power to deny Thomas' confirmation. This again speaks to the masculinity ascribed to places of political leadership. The claims of sexual harassment only bolster the masculinity of Thomas, indiscriminate of his race. This was seen as untenable to Moseley Braun and required some direct action.

Clarence Thomas went on to be confirmed to the U.S. Supreme Court on October 15, 1991, and Senator Allen Dixon of Illinois voted in favor (Apple, 1991). Carol Moseley Braun was the Recorder of Deeds in Cook County, which was rife with political corruption. Her efforts to right the ship was noticed by constituents who interfaced with the office. According to Moseley Braun, a letter encouraging her to run for Senate based upon the work she had done in Cooke County along with her state legislative career, made a bid of the chamber viable. Moseley Braun fits the characteristics of many other women of the CBC. She was committed to amplifying the voices of the voiceless, she was seen as a person with the ability to get things done, and she was not assuaged by those who had more resources. Her commitment to change is seen in a quote after she is elected to the Senate where she says, "Symbols will not create jobs and economic growth," she declared. "They do not do the hard work of solving the health care crisis. They will not save the children of our cities from drugs and guns and murder" (Nordgren, 1992).

In the Senate, Moseley Braun and Senator Dianne Feinstein of California became just the second and third women ever to serve on the influential Judiciary Committee. Moseley Braun also served on the Banking, Housing, and Urban Affairs Committee and on the Small Business Committee. In the 104th Congress (1995–1997), she became the first Democratic woman to serve on the powerful Finance Committee. In 1993, Moseley Braun waged a prolonged fight to prevent the renewal of a design patent for the United Daughters of the Confederacy (UDC) because it contained the Confederate flag. The patent had been routinely renewed for nearly a century, but Moseley Braun used her seat on the Judiciary Committee to strip the renewal provision from pending legislation.

Senator Moseley Braun's stance on this issue surrounding the confederate flag can be seen in the legislation she sponsored. In the 103rd Congress, she sponsored S.1975: Historically Black Colleges and Universities Historic Building Restoration and Preservation Act, which directed the

Secretary of the Interior to make grants to HBCUs for the preservation and restoration of historic buildings available through the National Historic Preservation Act of 1966. Or S. 2034: Education Infrastructure Act of 1994, which directed the Secretary of Education to award grants to eligible local educational agencies to meet the National Education Goals through repair, renovation, alteration, and construction of public elementary or secondary school libraries, media centers, or facilities. Moseley Braun's commitment to education was in many ways to dissuade the ignorance displayed in the acceptance of a confederate symbol.

In the 104th Congress, Senator Moseley Braun continued to sponsor legislation that advocated for those in vulnerable positions. This is seen with S.1756: Women's Pension Equity Act of 1996, which amended the Internal Revenue Code and the Employee Retirement Income Security Act of 1974 (ERISA) to allow fewer barriers for women to access retirement income, or S.746: Economic Opportunity and Family Responsibility Act of 1995, a comprehensive piece of legislation that amended several sections of the Social Security Act. The goal of the legislation was to increase job opportunities and basic skills training programs so that they better responded to the needs of the participants. The legislation was comprehensive as it addressed work-related reforms, treatment of teenage parents, parental responsibility, tax reforms for parents, child care reforms, and a host of equity investments. Although none of the previous legislation came to the Senate Floor, Senator Moseley Braun was successful in getting legislation passed in the chamber.

In the 103rd Congress, two pieces of legislation passed in the Senate with one becoming law. S.1685: DOE Minority Bank Preservation Act of 1993 amended the Federal Deposit Insurance Act to provide separate Federal deposit insurance for each beneficiary of an irrevocable trust or insured depository institution. The object of the legislation was to provide funding for wastewater treatment projects in minority communities. Senator Moseley Braun understood that improving infrastructure directly affected housing stock, and abating health hazards caused by groundwater contamination were needed more in minority communities. Senator Braun focused on sponsoring legislation that longitudinal effects on the Black communities that would improve the lives of Black people generationally.

Senator Moseley Braun was unafraid to verbally spare on the Senate Floor. This was first seen when Senator Jesse Helms prepared to approve the patent extension for the UDC. On July 22, 1993, Moseley Braun took to the Senate Floor to discuss race. During this almost 15-min speech, where the call for order on the floor was asked for numerous times, she stated, "this has no place in our modern times ... It has no place in the Senate ... it has no place in our society" (Moseley Braun, 2024).

Moseley Braun sparred with Senator Helms once more concerning federal funding for the Martin Luther King, Jr., Holiday. On May 23, 1994, H.R. 1933 was read on the Senate Floor (Congressional Record, 1994). The legislation, sponsored by John Lewis of Georgia's 4th district, authorized appropriations for the Martin Luther King, Jr., Federal Holiday Commission, to extend such commission, and to support the planning and performance of national service opportunities in conjunction with the federal legal holiday honoring the birthday of Martin Luther King, Jr. Helms' amendment to this legislation would have replaced government money with private donations not providing the commission with a reliable funding base. Moseley Braun thwarted Helms' effort and sponsored S.887: the National Underground Railroad Network to Freedom Act. The bill died in the chamber, but H.R. 1635: the National Underground Railroad Network to Freedom Act of 1998 sponsored by CBC member Louis Stokes became law.

Senator Moseley Braun's outspokenness came at a cost. She was initially accused of violating campaign finance regulations during her 1992 race. An investigation was carried out by the Federal Election Commission over the course of her first term. After 5 years, the charges were dismissed when only a minor discrepancy of $311 was found. Yet, the damage had been done. Due to the close scrutiny and lack of strong financial support from the Democratic Party, Moseley Braun lost her bid for reelection. The seat was returned to a White male Republican Peter G. Fitzgerald, an Illinois state senator who spent nearly $12 million of his own money on the campaign to win (Moseley Braun, 1994).

The experiences of the first Black woman to serve in the Senate mirror what the literature has illuminated. Women are to be soft-spoken and not to be perceived as aggressive. That women's concerns are not to be treated with any seriousness, and Black women's concerns should be ignored as they are irrational actors. That Black women can escape neither their Blackness nor their womanness, making their intersecting oppression visible and ever-present. Senator Moseley Braun's experiences even fall into the trope that Black people are not to be trusted. Yet, her example provided a road map for two other Black women: Kamala D. Harris became the second Black woman to serve in the Senate and Laphonza Butler was the third.

Laphonza Butler was appointed to the Senate on October 1, 2023. The Governor of California, Gavin Newsom, selected her to fill the seat left vacant by the death of Dianne Feinstein (California, 2024). Butler does not fit inside of the mold of previous CBC female legislators. She is married to Neneki Lee, making her the first open LGBT female CBC member; she never ran a campaign winning a government office at the local, state, or national level. Instead, she was politically adjacent leading in areas that were directly affected by policies championed in the legislature. A host of online biographies state that Butler is originally from Mississippi and graduated from Jackson State University, a HBCU, in political science.

When moving to California, she got rights to advocate for working people. For more than a decade, Butler served as the president of Service Employees International Union (SEIU) Local 2015. Local 2015 is the largest union representing more than 325,000 nursing home and home-care workers in California, and the largest long-term care union in the country. To maximize those she advocated for, Butler served as an SEIU International vice president and president of the SEIU California State Council. In addition, she has served as a board member for the National Children's Defense Fund, BLACK PAC, and the Bay Area Economic Council Institute, and was the former director for the Board of Governors of the Los Angeles branch of the Federal Reserve System.

Before being appointed to the Senate, Butler was president of EMILYs List. The organization name stands for the saying "Early Money is Like Yeast." The organization was founded in 1985 and has become the nation's largest resource for Democratic women in politics. As the president of this organization, Butler has ties to Senator Carol Moseley Braun. Senator Moseley Braun was elected in 1992 dubbed as the "Year of the Woman." In 1992, EMILYs List helped elect four new women senators and 20 new congresswomen. Their organizational membership grew substantially with more than 23,000 members contributing over $10.2 million. Butler has worked directly for the government; she was appointed by Governor Jerry Brown to the University California Board of Regents in August, 2018. She resigned in September 2021 from her 12-year term to take the helm at EMILYs List (2023).

Butlers' commitment to education and working-class people is seen in the legislation she sponsors. In the 118th Congress, she sponsors S.4903: Generation Now Workforce Representation Act of 2024, which improves workforce system planning and accountability; the bill ensures that Opportunity Youth and the organizations serving them are embedded into the structure of workforce boards around the country. Opportunity youth is a euphemism to describe young people who are between the ages of 16 and 24 years, are not attending school, and do not have jobs. As a union representative and a supervisor for a collegiate education system, Butler saw firsthand what the lack of investment created in American society.

In the 118th Congress, she went on to sponsor S.5031: Workforce of the Future Act of 2024. The bill authorizes the Secretary of Education to increase access to emerging and advanced technology education. The bill promotes a 21st-century artificial intelligence workforce upskilling workers preparing them for a technological future from prekindergarten through grade 12. Again, Butler uses her understanding of the educational systems and the workforce to propose legislation that would better prepare the people she spent her life advocating for. In this way, she is aligned with all the CBC female members before her. Although appointed rather than elected, Laphonza Butler has not waivered on her commitment to working-class people. Both pieces of legislation have not left their assigned committees, and with the least productive Congress since the Great Depression their success is tenuous.

Senator Butler has seen legislative victory with Senate Resolution 488 in the 118th Congress. Like many CBC women before her, Butler understood that the passing of a resolution was often the gateway for more substantial legislation. S.Res. 448 was a resolution supporting the goals and ideals of National Domestic Violence Awareness Month. The resolution was approved in a voice vote on the Senate floor leading to advocation for increased funding for domestic violence prevention programs. Like Congresswoman Cardiss Collins, Butler used her position in the U.S. Congress to bring attention to an issue that matter. Congresswoman Collins repetitively sponsored a resolution about breast cancer awareness in the month of October, making it a national focus. Unfortunately, Senator Butler will not have such an opportunity as she did not run for the Senate seat in which she was appointed. Although her tenure as a Black woman in the U.S. Senate was not lengthy, it was historic and directly speak to the long-standing relationship she has with Vice President Kamala Harris.

The Senate has been the gateway to the presidency for both Barack Obama and Kamala Harris. Both were junior Senators when they launched their presidential campaigns in 2008 and 2020, respectively. For Obama, it carried him to the White House as the 44th president of the United States who served two consecutive terms. Yet, Harris met an older White male in the Democratic primary who thwarted her chances, a former Senator Joseph R. Biden. President Biden fits as the prototypical citizen who can "legitimately" hold the Office of Presidency. He spent his entire adult life serving in the U.S. Senate before becoming vice president to Junior Senator Barack Obama. Biden's masculinity was rarely challenged until he was seen as impartial to Barack Obama in his second term in the White House. The book *The Long Alliance: The Imperfect Union of Joe Biden and Barack Obama* (Debenedetti, 2022) refutes the bromance decried by many in the media as feminization, which tried to make Biden an unviable presidential candidate.

Kamala Harris' journey to the U.S. Senate and later the Vice Presidency was complex; yet, she continued to fit inside of a mold laid before her by other women of the CBC. Kamala Devi Harris was born in Oakland, CA, two years before the founding of the Black Panther Party in 1966. Her parents were well educated, attending the University of California at Berkeley studying economics and biology, respectively. She went on to attend Howard University, a historically Black university in the nation's capital, graduating with a BA in political science in 1986. While there, she joined Alpha Kappa Alpha Sorority Incorporated, which is the oldest Black female Greek sorority.

She returned to the San Francisco Bay Area attending the University of California, Hastings College of the Law, where she served as president of its chapter of the Black Law Students Association (Kepley, 2019). After graduating in 1989, she began her law career as the district attorney of Alameda County. She grounded her career in law enforcement, in an effort to have the criminal justice system be more just. In this way, she fashioned herself after Stephanie Tubbs Jones who was a prosecutor in Cleveland, or Val Demings who was the first Black female police chief of Orlando.

Like many of those who came before her, Harris was not uncomfortable being the first. She was the first Black female district attorney of Alameda County; the first Black female elected district attorney of San Francisco in 2003; and the first Black female attorney general of California in 2010 and was reelected in 2014. Questions about her Blackness were always prevalent as her mother was an Indian immigrant. Yet, the Black community saw her as a leader that was fighting for the Black community. This is evident on February 25, 2006, when Kamala Harris took the seat of Congresswoman Shelia Jackson Lee at the State of the Black Union. In 2006, this annual event was held in Houston, TX; Harris took the seat of Lee during the Emerging Leaders panel as a symbolic gesture of those younger generations taking the torch. This was a national event that was seen by anyone who watched C-SPAN 1 during the prime-time hour (C-SPAN, 2006).

Harris was committed to repair in the criminal justice system clearing 27 of 74 backlogged homicide cases as district attorney of San Francisco (Soltau, 2004). She also pushed for higher bail for criminal defendants involved in gun-related crimes. She worked with San Francisco police officers to close historic loopholes defendants had used, such as lower bail in Black and Brown communities. She even kept a campaign promise not to seek the death penalty. This was difficult when San Francisco Police Department officer Isaac Espinoza was shot and killed by Edwin Ramos, an alleged MS-13 gang member and illegal immigrant. Harris commitment to criminal justice and its reform was evident as California's Attorney General. She launched the Division of Recidivism Reduction and Re-Entry and implemented the Back on Track LA program, which provided educational and job training opportunities for nonviolent offenders (Palta, 2014).

Therefore, Kamala Harris' commitments when she reached the U.S. Senate were clear. In the 115th Congress, she sponsored S.3178: Justice for Victims of Lynching Act of 2018, which specified that an offense involving lynching is a criminal civil rights violation. A violator is subject to criminal penalties: a prison term, a fine, or both. On December 19, 2018, the legislation passed Senate with an amendment by voice vote; yet it was sidelined in the House of Representatives and was never assigned to committee. Antilynching laws have been an issue for the CBC for decades, and the lack of congressional support especially in the Senate made legislation unviable. Yet, Harris was unrelenting, sponsoring the bill again in the 116th Congress where the legislation passed in the Senate, yet did not pass in the House.

Yet, the CBC saw victory in the 117th Congress when Bobby Rush sponsored H.R. 55: Emmett Till Antilynching Act. The bill was more detailed than the legislation brought by then Senator Harris, making lynching a federal hate crime offense. Specifically, the bill imposed criminal penalties on an individual who conspires to commit a hate crime offense that results in death or serious bodily injury, which includes kidnapping or aggravated sexual abuse. Senator Harris was unable to get the legislation over the finish line while in the Senate, but her ability to get a similar bill passed by voice vote in the Senate twice provided confirmation of success if passed in the House of Representatives. What is even more fitting is that the Emmett Till legislation was signed into law while Harris was serving as the first Black female vice president of the United States.

Senator Kamala Harris continued to sponsor legislation that advocated for Black people and women in particular; unfortunately, the following bills were never assigned to committee. In the 115th Congress, Harris sponsored S.1446: A bill to reauthorize the Historically Black Colleges and Universities Historic Preservation program, which amended the Omnibus Parks and Public Lands Management Act of 1996 to reauthorize Historically Black Colleges and Universities Historic Preservation Fund Grant Program for fiscal year 2018 through 2024. She tried again the 116th Congress without success, or S.2162: ENOUGH Act, which stands for Ending Nonconsensual Online User Graphic Harassment. The bill amended the federal criminal code to make it a crime to knowingly distribute an intimate visual depiction of an individual with the lack of proper consent. The legislation imposed criminal penalties, which included a fine, a prison term of up to five years, or both.

In the 116th Congress, Senator Harris sponsored more legislation that advocated for the issues that overwhelmingly affect Black communities. In the summer of 2019, she sponsored S.2227: MORE Act, with the acronym standing for Marijuana Opportunity Reinvestment and Expungement Act. Specifically, the bill removed marijuana from the list of scheduled substances under the Controlled Substances Act and eliminates criminal penalties for an individual who manufactures, distributes, or possesses marijuana. As a district attorney and as attorney general in California, Harris was vocal about the decriminalization of marijuana and how it disproportionately hurt Black and Brown communities. It was a comprehensive bill that did some major things such as replace statutory references to marijuana and marihuana with cannabis; establish a trust fund to support various programs and services for individuals and businesses in communities impacted by the war on drugs; impose a 5% tax on cannabis products and requires revenues to be deposited into the trust fund; and establish a process to expunge convictions and conduct sentencing review hearings related to federal cannabis offenses. The bill was not assigned to committee.

Later in the session, Harris sponsored two environmental bills that were aimed at providing the much needed infrastructure to address health concerns in Black communities S.2466 and S.4401. The Water Justice Act, S.2466, addressed affordable access to clean water. An investigation of the Flint Water Crisis was led by CBC member Elijah Cummings who was then chair of the Oversight and Accountability Committee. The investigation revealed failures at the state level but highlighted the resources that the EPA needed to prevent another crisis. Therefore, the bill sponsored by Senator Harris addressed the lack of federal funding by establishing and expanding programs related to drinking water infrastructure, water pollution control, water supply, water recycling, water efficiency, and conservation programs. Specifically, the bill provided $50 billion in supplemental appropriations in fiscal year 2020 to the EPA for the reduction of contaminants in drinking water. The next year she sponsored S.4401: Environmental Justice for All Act. The bill established several environmental justice requirements, advisory bodies, and programs to address the disproportionate adverse human health or environmental effects on communities of color, low-income communities, or tribal and indigenous communities. Neither of these bills were assigned to a committee.

Senator Harris like many female CBC women before her turned to Senate Resolutions to see some legislative success. In the 115th Congress, she sponsored three resolutions that drew attention to the realities of Black life in America—S.Res. 118: A resolution condemning hate crime and any other form of racism, religious or ethnic bias, discrimination, incitement to violence, or animus targeting a minority in the United States. The resolution called on federal law enforcement officials to work with state and local officials, to expeditiously investigate all credible reports of hate crimes and incidents and threats against minorities in the United States and bring the perpetrators to justice. This resolution was used to better monitor and prosecute hate crimes in the Biden Administration. S.Res. 317: A resolution celebrating the 40th anniversary of the Senate Black Legislative Staff Caucus and its achievements in the Senate, which highlighted the Black staff who are routinely ignored. S.Res. 409: A resolution honoring the dedication and courage of the Buffalo Soldiers, and the contributions they made to the National Park System and to military history in the United States and throughout the world.

Senator Harris may not have seen the legislative success she desired, but it did not stop her from being vocal about the issues related to democracy. On May 5, 2019, Harris said "voter suppression" prevented Democrats Stacey Abrams and Andrew Gillum from winning the 2018 gubernatorial elections in Georgia and Florida; Abrams lost by 55,000 votes and Gillum by 32,000. During Brett Kavanaugh's Supreme Court confirmation hearings, Senator Harris questioned him about his meeting with the law firm founded by Donald Trump's personal attorney, Marc Kasowitz. Harris continued to ask Kavanaugh about the said meeting in regard to the Mueller Investigation in which she did not receive an answer (C-SPAN, 2018). Harris went on to vote against the confirmation of Kavanaugh to the Supreme Court. On January 13, 2020, Harris delivered remarks on the floor of the Senate concerning Donald Trump and his impeachment trial (C-SPAN, 2020). In her 12-min remarks, she spoke about the integrity of the American justice system and the principle that nobody, including an incumbent president, is above the law. She later asked Senate Judiciary Chairman Lindsey Graham to halt all judicial nominations during the impeachment trial, to which Senator Graham acquiesced (Budryk, 2020). Harris voted to convict Trump on charges of abuse of power and obstruction of Congress.

On January 20, 2021, after an insurrection on Capitol Hill 2 weeks prior, Kamala Harris became the first Black female vice president. In her first official act as vice president she was able to swear in Georgia Senator Raphael Warnock, the first Black man to represent the original colony in the United States. When Harris took office, the 117th Congress's Senate was divided 50–50 between Republicans and Democrats. Therefore, she would frequent the chamber she had just left. Her tiebreaking votes were needed to ensure the Biden Administration would be able to pass key legislation. Her tiebreaking vote was needed only months after being sworn into office to pass the American Rescue Plan Act of 2021. No Senate Republicans voted for the legislation, which proposed a much needed stimulus package in the thralls of COVID-19. Although she had been unsuccessful in passing legislation she sponsored in the chamber, her tiebreaking votes in the Senate made her a powerful force. On December 5, 2023, she again cemented her place in history breaking the record for the most tiebreaking votes cast by a vice president.

Although Kamala Harris had been a trailblazer going further than any other female CBC member, she met her ceiling on November 5, 2024. After a poor debate performance in June 2024, serious questions about the viability of President Joseph Biden serving another 4 years as president became rapid. Before the Democratic Party convention in August, Biden decided not to seek his party's nomination for president and endorsed Kamala Harris. On August 22, 2024, Harris accepted the Democratic Party's nomination to run for president. This made her the first Black woman to become the presidential candidate from a major party. In many ways, she was following in the footsteps of Congresswoman Shirley Chisolm, a woman Harris admired, which is clear in her sponsorship of S. 728: A bill to direct the Joint Committee on the Library to obtain a statue of Shirley Chisholm for placement in the U.S. Capitol. Harris had seen and experienced the limits placed on her due to intersecting oppression. She was aware that the office of the presidency was masculine in nature and was careful not to feed into those stereotypes. Yet, as a Black woman she was not seen as a rational actor and could not be trusted to lead America.

Vice President Harris' unfortunate loss proves the need for the CBC in 1971 and today. The Caucus was founded because its members needed to be in the Democratic Party but not of the Democratic Party. The ability to unabashedly advocate for the issues that matter most to Black communities was only viable with a separate entity that was not bound by party rules. Members of the CBC needed the space and room to create their own rules to exist and progress in the racialized structure of the Congress. The women of this Caucus have been committed to relentless advocation indiscriminate of their geographical location, collegiate alma mater, or personal idiosyncrasies. They used their visibility in their communities to gain the necessary trust to transcend the U.S. legislature. Such transcendence makes them a group of legislators who no longer are invisible to the larger legislative structure. Instead, they have used their radical imaginations to hoist a Black woman to the top of the Democratic Party ticket. When thinking about the women of the Congressional Black Caucus it is safe to say they have shone light into the legislative darkness.

# CHAPTER 7
## Black Women and Resolute Legislative Activism

Black women of the CBC have needed to be highly visible in their districts and in their states to be eligible for political post in the federal legislature. Their radical imagination about what the country could be continued to fuel these women generation after generation. These women have shown that they are prepared to be the lone voice of opposition in the House of Representatives, which often cast them into the harsh spotlight. A spotlight that confirms their invisibility in the larger legislative body, while simultaneously confirming their commitment to give the voiceless a voice. This has been a pillar of consciousness for members of the CBC since its founding; yet, Black women serve with a double-minority status making their intersecting oppressions visible and undeniable.

The first six chapters discuss the visibility alongside the invisibility of the women of the CBC qualitatively. It was in this review that a pattern was discovered. Black women were a small fraction of the 435 members in the House of Representatives, yet they consistently sponsored more bills than other affinity groups in the House. Black women substantively and over their time in Congress sponsored more legislation than other race–gender groups, particularly White men, in order to get their legislative agenda passed. This is definitely the case of Cardiss Collins, a foundational woman of the Caucus who represented Illinois 7th district.

Congresswoman Collins served for over 20 years sponsoring 466 bills and cosponsoring 4,918 bills, while being the only Black woman in Congress for 6 years from the 98th Congress to the 101st.

Black women's immense sponsorship serves as an invisible action, which receives little attention from their peers or the media, leading to visible outcomes of signature legislation being passed, even if they did not sponsor the legislation. This phenomenon is called resolute legislative activism: Black women's determination not to allow their intersecting oppressions to hinder the visibility and viability of their legislative agendas. This is an extension of the legislative activism the CBC has holistically used to be seen and heard around Black interest (Nelson, 2022). To best support this newly established theoretical framework, the following research questions were formulated:

1   Is the observed heightened legislative sponsorship by the women of the CBC a statistically significant observation?
2   Why did the women of the CBC engage in exorbitant legislative sponsorship?

A quantitative explanation alone would not be sufficient in answering these prevalent questions. Therefore, John Creswell's (2014) explanatory sequential design is used to answer these research questions and undergird the theory. Creswell's design was chosen as it uses a mixed-methods approach that rests on some quantitative analysis but needs qualitative data to interpret the quantitative outputs.

In the exploration of preliminary quantitative data connected to sponsorship and cosponsorship, Black women sponsored more bills than other gender–race groups. To best understand why this is the case, Tie et al.'s (2019) use of grounded theory is appropriate for explaining the behavior of these Black women. The flexibility of this theory allows the data to determine which steps are necessary to be included in the analysis. This framework allows for quantitative and qualitative data because it aims to "generate theory grounded in the data" (Tie et al., 2019, p. 2). It is for this reason that purposeful sampling was done collecting all the bills sponsored by all the Black and White male and female members of the House of Representative from the 93rd Congress to the 118th Congress.

This dataset was constructed by accumulating all the names of the members of the House of Representatives using the relevant information from the Library of Congress website, www.congress.gov. Every public house bill (H.R.) that was introduced into the 93rd to 117th Congresses (1973–2024) was recorded, and the sponsor for that bill was identified. Due to the lack of Black women who served in the Senate, Black CBC women were excluded from the dataset. The gender and race for each of these individuals was coded and those who identified as Latino or Asian solely were excluded. This was done to establish a racial binary as gender was the driver of the analysis. It also allowed for consistency throughout the 50-year analysis; in the 93rd Congress, there were only four representatives that identified as Latino and they were all men.

The use of purposeful sampling provided some keen observations. White men in the 93rd Congress sponsored 19,503 bills; in the 94th Congress, 17,744; in the 95th Congress, 16,349; yet, in the 96th Congress there is a precipitous drop to 9,524 bills. White men do not sponsor more than 8,400 bills collectively after the 96th Congress. Craig Volden and Alan E. Wiseman (2014) would argue that this is in support of White males being focused on legislative effectiveness. Their work *Legislative Effectiveness in the United States Congress: The Lawmakers* develops a methodology for scoring the lawmaking effectiveness of each member of Congress. They assert that the score identifies how lawmakers could better address the nation's policy problems. This method tracks a representative's legislation through each major stage of bill progression throughout the entirety of the legislation's life cycle. This progression includes the success of bills leaving one congressional chamber and becoming law.

The issue of the legislative effectiveness score when evaluating the heightened legislative sponsorship by the women of the CBC is twofold. First, the method does not ground itself in the inherent racialization of the formation of Congress. The creation of two separate chambers is directly connected to the unwillingness to grant Blacks citizenship and thus equal representation. This is exacerbated by the absence of women in Congress until the early 1900s. Jeannette Rankin, a Republican from Montana, became the first woman ever to be elected to Congress. She served in the U.S. House of Representatives from 1917 to 1919 and again from 1941 to 1942 (Center for American Women and Politics). Therefore, it would be irresponsible to use a metric committed to overall effectiveness when Blacks and women were originally barred access to the legislative body.

The second hindrance is the score's aim to better address the nation's policy problems. The interests of Black people are not always viewed as policy issues that need to be addressed by the nation. This is evident in the founding of the CBC moving away from being known as the Democratic Select Committee. Blatant ties to the major party did not allow the original 13 members the latitude they needed to advocate for Black interest. This phenomenon has not reduced over time but instead has morphed; William Julius Wilson (1997) discusses this in his book *When Work Disappears: The World of the New Urban Poor.* Before the turn of the century, racial discord and the growing racial divide between the city and the suburbs had grown substantially. In discussing these problems, there is a tendency to engage in rhetoric that exacerbates, rather than alleviates these tensions. These tensions are not often seen as national issues; therefore, legislation-sponsored design to address particular portions of this issue is unlikely to be successful. Therefore, purposeful sampling with the use of grounded theory produced sampling that allowed comparative analysis that followed the evidence.

When conducting this observational comparative analysis, there was a focus on the frequency of bills sponsored by Black women. Cosponsorship was not included in the analysis as the legislative strategy for the CBC changed over time. In the beginning, Caucus members refrained from sponsoring legislation together as it would flag the legislation as being primarily a Black issue that would not translate into legislative success. Instead, members were encouraged to find White male members in particular a White member with a similar issue in their district who could provide the CBC member support (Nelson, 2022). However, as time went on, the membership of the Caucus grew and this strategy was reimagined. Cosponsorship among the members of the CBC increased once they reached saliency saturating all the standing committees in Congress.

The dependent variable was bill sponsorship with the independent variable being the oppressive interactive effect of race and sex. In this dataset, the bills sponsored by Black members (the CBC) only compose 7.75 of all bills sponsored with a total of 865 sponsored pieces of legislation, while the bills sponsored by female members of Congress only compose 12.23 of all sponsored bills with a total of 1,365 pieces of legislation.

Initial frequencies show that Black women of the CBC have sponsored a total of 266 compared with the 10,892 sponsored by others (Figure 7.1).

| RECODE of K2 (Race (Binary)) | RECODE of I2 (Sex) | | Total |
|---|---|---|---|
| | Male | Female | |
| Not Black | 9,194 | 1,099 | 10,293 |
| Black | 599 | 266 | 865 |
| Total | 9,793 | 1,365 | 11,158 |

**Figure 7.1**  Bill Sponsorship in Racial Binary

Of the 11,000+ bills sponsored in this dataset, the mean is 21 with a standard deviation of 20.32. The min. is zero sponsored bills (85 persons sponsored no bills, and the max. is 324 sponsored bills). At first observation, the heightened legislative sponsorship by the women of the CBC is not seen as statistically significant.

However, Polluck's (2012) comparative analysis methodology is used to see whether the bill sponsorship by Black women is significant compared with the sponsorship of the rest of Congress. Because bill sponsorship is a continuous variable, values have an order and are equal units of measurement from one unit to the next. Subsequently, a comparison of the means was used instead of direct numbers or percentages. An interactive variable that combines race and gender, where "1" represents bills sponsored by Black women and "0" represents all other bills sponsored, is created. However, again, because bill sponsorship is a continuous variable, it would be more appropriate to compare the means. The mean sponsorship for Black women is 23.82, and the mean sponsorship for all others is 20.95. Clear evidence is that, on average, Black women are sponsoring more bills than the collective of Congress (Figure 7.2).

| | Mean |
|---|---|
| Racesex | |
| 0 | 20.95371 |
| 1 | 23.82632 |
| Total | 21.02222 |

**Figure 7.2**  Bill Sponsorship Mean

The following primary research question is not yet fully satisfied: Is the observed heightened legislative sponsorship by the women of the CBC a statistically significant observation? A two-sample *t*-test was operationalized to determine whether there is significance between Black CBC women and the rest of the House of Representatives. The output provides a *p*-value of .02, noting statistical significance for CBC women in the difference of the means at the .95 thresholds (Figure 7.3).

| Group | Obs | Mean | Std.err. | Std.dev. | [95% conf.interval] | |
|---|---|---|---|---|---|---|
| 0 | 10,888 | 20.95371 | .1948329 | 20.32996 | 20.5718 | 21.33562 |
| 1 | 266 | 23.82632 | 1.196766 | 19.51866 | 21.46994 | 26.1827 |
| Combined | 11,154 | 21.02222 | .1923529 | 20.31487 | 20.64517 | 21.39926 |
| diff | | −2.872605 | 1.260471 | | −5.343351 | −.4018591 |

diff = mean(0) − mean(1)                                          t = −2.2790

HO: diff = 0                                                      Degrees of freedom = 11152

Ha: diff < 0                    Ha: diff != 0                     Ha: diff > 0

Pr(T < t) = 0.0113             Pr(|T| > |t|) = 0.0227             Pr(T > t) = 0.9887

**Figure 7.3**   Two-Sample t-Test Comparing Entire House to Black CBC Women

With the question concerning statistical significance answered, the question about why these Black women engage in exorbitant legislative sponsorship still remains. There is limited scholarship on the issue of bill sponsorship particularly for women. Yet, Barnello and Bratton (2007) explored the conditions under which men are likely to focus attention on policy areas involving women's and children's issues. They examined the sponsorship of legislation in the upper and lower chambers of 15 state legislatures in 2001. What they found was quite fascinating: institutional context (such as party control of the legislature or diversity within the legislature) had little effect on the sponsorship behavior of either men or women. However, personal characteristics such as race, education, age, and family circumstances are associated with sponsorship by men.

Therefore, women who are often in the minority in the state and the federal legislature tend to make sponsorship decisions in spite of, but not because of, their diminutive status.

This is not at all surprising as Black women are concerned with the political representation of the least of these. These women recognize their elite status and have historically used their elevation to fight for democracy itself. From Congresswoman Barbara Jordan to Congresswoman Jasmine Crockett, there is a historical thread of legislation that is resolute in making America live up to her aims. The broader study of intersectionality is complex; it requires scholars to use different methodological approaches to examine the hurdles Black women, and in particular Black female CBC legislators, face. Many of the Black women discussed in this work have been the first and have overcome the struggles that make it difficult for them to declare candidacies, let alone win. Yet, these women have used their radical imaginations in legislative service to a country that does not love them back.

Their strategy had been clear: resolute legislative activism forces the larger legislative body to acknowledge their existence. This very determination was seen on January 3, 2025, when Stacey Plaskett, delegate for the U.S. Virgin Islands, stood and stated "I have a voice!" (J. Jones, 2025). Plaskett made a parliamentary inquiry to ask the House parliamentarian to explain why the six nonvoting delegates from U.S. territories and the District of Columbia aren't allowed to vote for speaker. Her inquiry highlighted the lack of representation of over 4 million primarily Black and Brown U.S. citizens. When the legislative floor is not available, Black CBC women have been busy sponsoring and cosponsoring bills in an effort to be visible to their colleagues and the American people.

Recognizing both the distinct intersectional challenges and opportunities for expanding Black women's political representation, there are a few recommendations for young Black women who aspire to follow in the footsteps of the women discussed in this book.

1. *Engage the community at all levels.* It is never too early to become involved in local politics. Attend civic forums like city council and schoolboard meetings; you will learn who has power and how that power is used to achieve a desired result.

2. *Find a mentor.* When attending these civic forms speak to those you don't know. Show interest in the agenda and have informed opinions. Most of the women in the CBC started as a pillar in their community, and those politically connected saw their potential and guided them through.

3. *Join a sorority.* Although many doubt the sincerity of and the modern-day relevance of sororities, they are often 100-year-old institutions. Your membership will teach you about politics and power dynamics that replicate themselves across the political landscape. It will help increase your network of other influential women, and will help you mobilize voters, secure key endorsements and campaign donations when running for office.

4. *Join and engage Civil Rights Organizations.* Although the strength and viability of these organizations have shifted, legacy organizations like the National Associate for the Advancement of Colored People (NAACP), the National Council of Negro Women (NCNW), the National Action Network, or the National Urban League are often the first places those in the political environment come to understand Black issues.

5. *Support Black women currently running for office.* You can always volunteer your time in the political office of Black women. Black women are often short-staffed as they do not have the financial resources of their counterparts. Therefore, volunteering in their office and on the campaign trail consistently will get you noticed.

6. *Engage Black and Female Political Action Committees (PACs).* The *Citizens United v. Federal Election Commission* in 2010 allowed corporations including for-profits, nonprofit organizations, labor unions, and other associations First Amendment rights in regards to independent expenditures for political campaigns. Simply it allowed those with an absorbent number of resources to spend freely on political campaigns. Consequently, women groups and well-connected Blacks have organized some political action committees to help financially support candidates; they are Black PAC, Black Economic Alliance PAC, The Collective PAC, and National Organization for Women PAC.

7.  *Find a Candidate Training Program.* Once you commit to the former things on this list, seek a training program. Oftentimes, these training programs are connected to PACs, which create pipelines into particular political environments. The training is often available at your skill and engagement level, as running for mayor in a small town is different than running for the state legislature. The Congressional Black Caucus Institute has a training as well as the Collective PAC, EMILYs List, and EMERGE.

# Appendix

## Alphabetical Listing of Congressional Black Caucus Members' (93rd–118th) Congresses

*Including Dates of Service and Committee Assignments*

**ADAMS, ALMA S.** Democrat; North Carolina, 12th District. Elected to the 113th Congress to fill the vacancy caused by the resignation of Melvin L. Watt, and also elected to the 114th–115th Congresses (served November 4, 2014–present)

Committee assignments:

- H. Agriculture (114th–115th Congresses)
- H. Education and the Workforce (114th–115th Congresses)
- H. Small Business (114th–115th Congresses)

**BASS, KAREN.** Democrat, California, 33rd (112th Congress) and 37th District (113th Congress—present). Elected to the 112th–115th Congresses (served January 3, 2011–present)

Committee assignments:

- H. Budget (112th Congress)
- H. Foreign Affairs (112th–115th Congresses)
- H. Judiciary (113th–115th Congresses)

**BEATTY, JOYCE.** Democrat, Ohio, 3rd District. Elected to the 113th–115th Congresses (served January 3, 2013–present)

Committee assignments:

- H. Financial Services (113th–115th Congresses)

**BLUNT ROCHESTER, LISA.** Democrat; Delaware, At-Large. Elected to the 115th Congress (served January 3, 2017–present)

Committee assignments:

- H. Agriculture (115th Congress)
- H. Education and the Workforce (115th Congress)

**BROWN, CORRINE.** Democrat; Florida, 3rd District (103rd–112th Congresses), 5th District (113th–114th Congress). Elected to the 103rd–114th Congresses (served January 3, 1993–January 3, 2017)

Committee assignments:

- H. Government Operations (103rd Congress)
- H. Public Works and Transportation (103rd Congress)
- H. Transportation and Infrastructure (104th–114th Congresses)
- H. Veterans' Affairs (103rd–114th Congresses; ranking member, 114th Congress)

**BROWN, SHONTEL MONIQUE.** Democrat; Ohio, 11th District (117th Congress—present)

Committee assignments:

- H. Agriculture
- H. Oversight and Reform
- United States House Select Committee on Strategic Competition between the United States and the Chinese Communist Party

**BURKE, YVONNE BRATHWAITE.** Democrat; California, 28th (94th–95th Congresses) and 37th (93rd Congress) Districts. Elected to the 93rd–95th Congresses (served January 3, 1973–January 3, 1979). First female chair of the Congressional Black Caucus, 94th–95th Congresses

Committee assignments:

- H. Public Works (93rd Congress)
- H. Interior and Insular Affairs (93rd Congress)
- H. Appropriations (94th–95th Congresses)
- H. Select Committee on the House Beauty Shop (chair, 94th–95th Congresses)

**BUSH, CORI.** Democrat; Missouri, 1st District (117th–118th Congresses)
Committee assignments:

- H. Committee on Oversight and Accountability
- H. Committee on the Judiciary

**CARSON, JULIA.** Democrat; Indiana, 10th District (105th–107th Congresses) and 7th District (108th–110th Congresses). Elected to the 105th–110th Congresses (served January 3, 1997 until her death December 15, 2007).
Committee assignments:

- H. Banking and Financial Services/Financial Services (105th–110th Congresses)
- H. Veterans' Affairs (105th–107th Congresses)
- H. Transportation and Infrastructure (108th–110th Congresses)

**CHERFILUS-MCCORMICK, SHELIA.** Democrat; Florida, 20th District (117th Congress—present)
Committee assignments:

- H. Foreign Affairs
- H. Veteran Affairs

**CHISHOLM, SHIRLEY ANITA.** Democrat; New York, 12th District. Elected to the 91st to 97th Congresses (served January 3, 1969–January 3, 1983)
Committee assignments:

- H. Veterans' Affairs (91st–92nd Congresses)
- H. Education and Labor (92nd–94th Congresses)
- H. Rules (95th–97th Congresses)

**CHRISTENSEN, DONNA.** Democrat; Delegate from the Virgin Islands. Elected to the 105th–113th Congresses (served January 3, 1997–January 3, 2015)

Committee assignments:

- H. Resources/Natural Resources (105th–112th Congresses)
- H. Small Business (105th–109th Congresses)
- H. Homeland Security (108th–110th Congresses; 112th Congress)
- H. Energy and Commerce (111th–113th Congresses)

**CLARKE, YVETTE.** Democrat; New York, 11th District (110th–112th Congresses) and 9th District (113th Congress—present). Elected to the 110th–115th Congresses (served January 3, 2007–present)

Committee assignments:

- H. Education and Labor (110th–111th Congresses)
- H. Homeland Security (110th–113th Congresses)
- H. Small Business (110th–114th Congresses)
- H. Ethics (113th–115th Congresses)
- H. Energy and Commerce (114th–115th Congresses)

**CLAYTON, EVA.** Democrat; North Carolina, 1st District. Elected to the 102nd Congress November 3, 1992, to fill vacancy caused by death of Walter Jones; simultaneously elected to the 103rd Congress; reelected to the 104th–107th Congresses (served November 5, 1992–January 3, 2003)

Committee assignments:

- H. Agriculture (103rd–107th Congresses)
- H. Small Business (103rd–104th Congresses)
- H. Budget (105th–107th Congresses)

**COLLINS, BARBARA-ROSE.** Democrat; Michigan, 13th District (102nd Congress) and 15th District (103rd–104th Congresses). Elected to the 102nd–104th Congresses (served January 3, 1991–January 3, 1997)

Committee assignments:

- H. Public Works and Transportation (102nd–103rd Congresses)
- H. Science, Space and Technology (102nd Congress)

- H. Government Operations (103rd Congress)
- H. Post Office and Civil Service (103rd Congress)
- H. Government Reform and Oversight (104th Congress)
- H. Transportation and Infrastructure (104th Congress)
- H. Select Children, Youth, and Families (102nd Congress)

**COLLINS, CARDISS.** Democrat; Illinois, 7th District. Elected to the 93rd Congress in a June 5, 1973, special election to fill vacancy caused by death of husband George W. Collins; reelected to the 94th–104th Congresses (served June 7, 1973–January 3, 1997). Chair of the Congressional Black Caucus, 96th Congress.

Committee assignments:

- H. Government Operations/Government Reform and Oversight (93rd–104th Congresses)
- H. International Relations/Foreign Affairs (94th–96th Congresses)
- H. District of Columbia (95th Congress)
- H. Select Committee on Narcotics Abuse and Control (96th–102nd Congresses)
- H. Energy and Commerce/Commerce (97th–104th Congresses)

**CROCKETT, JASMINE FELICIA.** Democrat; Texas, 30th District 117th Congress—present

Committee assignments:

- H. Agriculture
- H. Oversight and Accountability

**DEMINGS, VAL.** Democrat; Florida, 10th District. Elected to the 115th Congress (served January 3, 2017–present)

Committee assignments:

- H. Homeland Security (115th Congress)
- H. Government Reform (115th Congress)
- H. Judiciary (115th Congress)

**EDWARDS, DONNA.** Democrat; Maryland, 4th District. Elected to the 110th Congress in a June 17, 2008, special election to fill vacancy caused by the resignation of Albert Wynn; reelected to the 111th–114th Congresses (served June 19, 2008–January 3, 2017)

Committee assignments:

- H. Science and Technology/Science, Space and Technology (110th–114th Congresses)
- H. Transportation and Infrastructure (110th–114th Congresses)
- H. Ethics (112th Congress)

**FOUSHEE, VALERIE JEAN.** Democrat; North Carolina's, 4th District 117th Congress—present
Committee assignments:

- H. Transportation and Infrastructure
- H. Oversight and Accountability

**FUDGE, MARCIA F.** Democrat; Ohio, 11th District. Elected to the 110th Congress in a November 4, 2008, special election to fill vacancy caused by death of Stephanie Tubbs Jones; reelected to the 111th–115th Congresses (served November 19, 2008–present). Chair of the Congressional Black Caucus, 113th Congress.
Committee assignments:

- H. Education and Labor/Education and the Workforce (111th Congress; 113th–115th Congresses)
- H. Science and Technology/Science, Space and Technology (111th–112th Congresses)
- H. Agriculture (112th–115th Congresses)

**HALL, KATIE BEATRICE.** Democrat; Indiana, 1st District. Elected to the 97th Congress in a Nov. 2, 1982, special election to fill vacancy caused by death of Adam Benjamin Jr.; reelected to the 98th Congress (served November 29, 1982–January 3, 1985)
Committee assignments:

- H. Post Office and Civil Service (98th Congress)
- H. Public Works and Transportation (98th Congress)

**HARRIS, KAMALA DEVI.** Democrat; California, Senator. Elected in 2016 (served January 3, 2017–present)

Committee assignments:

- S. Budget (115th Congress)
- S. Environment and Public Works (115th Congress)
- S. Homeland Security (115th Congress)
- S. Judiciary (115th Congress)
- S. Select Intelligence (115th Congress)

**HAYES, JAHANA.** Democrat; Connecticut, 5th District. Elected to the 116th Congress (served January 3, 2019–present)

Committee assignments:

- H. Education and Labor (116th Congress)
- H. Agriculture (116th Congress)

**JACKSON LEE, SHEILA.** Democrat; Texas, 18th District. Elected to the 104th–115th Congresses (served January 3, 1995–2024)

Committee assignments:

- H. Judiciary (104th–115th Congresses)
- H. Science (104th–109th Congresses)
- H. Homeland Security (108th–115th Congresses)
- H. Foreign Affairs (110th–111th Congresses)

**JOHNSON, EDDIE BERNICE.** Democrat; Texas, 30th District. Elected to the 103rd–115th Congresses (served January 3, 1993–present). Chair of the Congressional Black Caucus, 107th Congress.

Committee assignments:

- H. Public Works and Transportation (103rd Congress)
- H. Science, Space, and Technology/Science/Science and Technology (103rd–115th Congresses; ranking member, 112th–115th Congresses)
- H. Transportation and Infrastructure (104th–115th Congresses)

**JONES, BRENDA.** Democrat; Michigan, 13th District. Elected to the 115th Congress in a November 6, 2018, special election to fill vacancy caused by resignation of John Conyers (served November 29, 2018–January 3, 2019)

No committee assignments listed.

**JONES, STEPHANIE TUBBS.** Democrat; Ohio, 11th District. Elected to the 106th–110th Congresses (served January 3, 1999 until her death on August 20, 2008)

Committee assignments:

- H. Banking and Financial Services (106th Congress)
- H. Financial Services (107th Congress)
- H. Small Business (106th–107th Congresses)
- H. Standards of Official Conduct (107th–110th Congresses; chair, 110th Congress)
- H. Ways and Means (108th–110th Congresses)

**JORDAN, BARBARA C.** Democrat; Texas, 18th District. Elected to the 93rd–95th Congresses (served January 3, 1973–January 3, 1979)

Committee assignments:

- H. Judiciary (93rd–95th Congresses)
- H. Government Operations (94th–95th Congresses)

**KAMLAGER-DOVE, SYDNEY KAI.** Democrat; California's, 37th District 118th Congress—present

Committee assignments:

- H. Foreign Affairs
- H. Natural Resources

**KELLY, ROBIN.** Democrat; Illinois, 2nd District. Elected to the 113th Congress in an April 9, 2013, special election to vacancy caused by resignation of Jesse Jackson Jr.; reelected to the 114th–115th Congresses (served April 11, 2013–present)

Committee assignments:

- H. Oversight and Government Reform (113th–115th Congresses)
- H. Science, Space, and Technology (113th Congress)
- H. Foreign Affairs (114th–115th Congresses)

**KILPATRICK, CAROLYN CHEEKS.** Democrat; Michigan, 15th District (105th–107th Congresses) and 13th District (108th–111th Congresses). Elected to the 105th–111th Congresses (served January 3, 1997–January 3, 2011). Chair of the Congressional Black Caucus, 110th Congress.

Committee assignments:

- H. Banking and Financial Services (105th Congress)
- H. House Oversight (105th Congress)
- Jt. Library (105th Congress)
- H. Appropriations (106th–111th Congresses)

**LAWRENCE, BRENDA L.** Democrat; Michigan, 14th District. Elected to the 114th–115th Congress (served January 3, 2015–present)

Committee assignments:

- H. Oversight and Government Reform (114th–115th Congresses)
- H. Small Business (114th Congress)
- H. Transportation and Infrastructure (115th Congress)

**LEE, BARBARA.** Democrat; California, 9th District. Elected to the 105th Congress in an April 7, 1998, special election to fill vacancy caused by resignation of Ronald Dellums; reelected to the 106th–115th Congresses (served April 20, 1998–2025). Chair of the Congressional Black Caucus, 111th Congress.

Committee assignments:

- H. Banking and Financial Services (105th–106th Congresses)
- H. Financial Services (107th–109th Congresses)
- H. Science (105th Congress)
- H. International Relations (107th–109th Congresses)

- H. Foreign Affairs (110th–111th Congresses)
- H. Appropriations (110th–115th Congresses)
- H. Budget (113th–115th Congresses)

**LEE, SUMMER L.** Democrat; Pennsylvania, 12th District 118th Congress—present

Committee assignments:

- H. Science and Technology
- H. Oversight and Accountability

**LOVE, MIA B.** Republican; Utah, 4th District. Elected to the 114th–115th Congress (served Jan. 3, 2015–2019)

Committee assignment:

- H. Financial Services (114th–115th Congresses)

**MAJETTE, DENISE L.** Democrat; Georgia, 4th District. Elected to the 108th Congress (served January 3, 2003–January 3, 2005)

Committee assignments:

- H. Budget (108th Congress)
- H. Education and the Workforce (108th Congress)
- H. Small Business (108th Congress)

**MCBATH, LUCY.** Democrat; Georgia, 6th District. Elected to the 116th Congress (served January 3, 2019–present)

Committee assignments:

- H. Judiciary (116th Congress)
- H. Education and Labor (116th Congress)

**MCCLELLAN, JENNIFER LEIGH** Democrat; Virginia, 4th District (118th Congress—present)

Committee assignments:

- H. Armed Services
- H. Science, Space, and Technology

**MCKINNEY, CYNTHIA.** Democrat; Georgia, 11th District (103rd–104th Congresses) and 4th District (105th–107th Congress and 109th Congress).

Elected to the 103rd to 107th Congresses and to the 109th Congress (served January 3, 1993–January 3, 2003; January 3, 2005–January 3, 2007)

Committee assignments:

- H. Agriculture (103rd–104th Congresses)
- H. Foreign Affairs (103rd Congress)
- H. Banking and Finance (104th–105th Congresses)
- H. International Relations (104th–107th Congresses)
- H. National Security (105th Congress)
- H. Armed Services (106th–107th Congresses; 109th Congress)
- H. Budget (109th Congress)

**MEEK, CARRIE.** Democrat; Florida, 17th District. Elected to the 103rd to 107th Congresses (served January 3, 1993–January 3, 2003)

Committee assignments:

- H. Appropriations (103rd Congress; 105th–107th Congresses)
- H. Budget (104th Congress)
- H. Government Reform and Oversight (104th Congress)

**MILLENDER-McDONALD, JUANITA.** Democrat; California, 37th District. Elected to the 104th Congress in a March 26, 1996, special election to fill vacancy caused by resignation of Walter Tucker; reelected to the 105th–110th Congresses (served April 16, 1996 until her death on April 22, 2007)

Committee assignments:

- H. Small Business (104th–110th Congresses)
- H. Transportation and Infrastructure (104th–110th Congresses)
- H. Administration (108th–110th Congresses; ranking member, 109th Congress; chair, 110th Congress)
- Jt. Library (108th–110th Congresses)
- Jt. Printing (109th–110th Congresses)

**MOORE, GWENDOLYNNE (GWEN).** Democrat; Wisconsin, 4th District. Elected to the 109th–115th Congresses (served January 3, 2005–present)

Committee assignments:

- H. Financial Services (109th–115th Congresses)
- H. Small Business (109th–111th Congresses)
- H. Budget (110th–114th Congresses)

**MOSELEY BRAUN, CAROL.** Democrat; Illinois, Senator. Elected in 1992 (served January 3, 1993–January 3, 1999)
Committee assignments:

- S. Banking, Housing, and Urban Affairs (103rd–105th Congresses)
- S. Judiciary (103rd Congress)
- S. Small Business (103rd Congress)
- S. Finance (104th–105th Congresses)
- S. Special Aging (104th–105th Congresses)

**NORTON, ELEANOR HOLMES.** Democrat; Delegate from the District of Columbia. Elected to the 102nd–115th Congresses (served January 3, 1991–present)
Committee assignments:

- H. District of Columbia (102nd–103rd Congresses)
- H. Post Office and Civil Service (102nd–103rd Congresses)
- H. Public Works and Transportation (102nd–103rd Congresses)
- Jt. Committee on the Organization of Congress (103rd Congresses)
- H. Small Business (104th Congress)
- H. Oversight and Government Reform/Government Reform (104th–115th Congresses)
- H. Transportation and Infrastructure (104th–115th Congresses)
- H. Homeland Security (108th–111th Congresses)

**OMAR, ILHAN.** Democrat; Minnesota, 5th District. Elected to the 116th Congress (served January 3, 2019–present)
Committee assignments:

- H. Budget (116th Congress)
- H. Foreign Affairs (116th Congress)
- H. Education and Labor (116th Congress)

**PRESSLEY, AYANNA.** Democrat; Massachusetts, 7th District. Elected to the 116th Congress (served January 3, 2019–present)

Committee assignments:

- H. Financial Services (116th Congress)
- H. Oversight Reform (116th Congress)

**PLASKETT, STACEY E.** Democrat; Delegate from the U.S. Virgin Islands. Elected to the 114th Congress (served January 3, 2015–present)

Committee assignments:

- H. Agriculture (114th–115th Congresses)
- H. Oversight and Government Reform (114th–115th Congresses)

**RICHARDSON, LAURA.** Democrat, California, 37th District. Elected to the 110th Congress in an August 21, 2007, special election to fill vacancy caused by death of Juanita Millender-McDonald; reelected to the 111th–112th Congresses (served September 4, 2007–January 3, 2013)

Committee assignments:

- H. Science and Technology (110th Congress)
- H. Transportation and Infrastructure (110th–112th Congresses)
- H. Homeland Security (111th–112th Congresses)

**SEWELL, TERRYCINA ("TERRI").** Democrat; Alabama, 7th District. Elected to the 112th–115th Congresses (served January 3, 2011–present)

Committee assignments:

- H. Agriculture (112th Congress)
- H. Science, Space and Technology (112th Congress)
- H. Financial Services (113th–114th Congresses)
- H. Intelligence (113th–115th Congresses)
- H. Ways and Means (115th Congress)

**SYKES, EMILIA STRONG** Democrat; Ohio's, 13th District (118th Congress—present)

Committee assignments

- H. Space, Science, and Technology
- H. Transportation and Infrastructure

**STRICKLAND, MARILYN.** Democrat; Washington, 10th District. Elected to the 117th Congress—present

Committee assignments:

- H. Armed Services
- H. Transportation and Infrastructure

**UNDERWOOD, LAUREN.** Democrat; Illinois, 14th District. Elected to the 116th Congress (served January 3, 2019–present)

Committee assignments:

- H. Education and Labor (116th Congress)
- H. Veterans' Affairs (116th Congress)
- H. Homeland Security (116th Congress)

**WATERS, MAXINE.** Democrat; California, 29th District (102nd Congress), 35th District (103rd–112th Congresses) and 43rd District (113th Congress—present). Elected to the 102nd to 116th Congresses (served January 3, 1991–present) Chair, Congressional Black Caucus, 105th Congress. Chair H. Financial Services

Committee assignments:

- H. Banking, Finance, and Urban Affairs/Banking and Financial Services (102nd–106th Congresses)
- H. Financial Services (107th–116th Congresses; ranking member, 113th–116th Congresses)
- H. Veterans' Affairs (102nd–104th Congresses)
- H. Small Business (103rd–104th Congresses)
- H. Judiciary (105th–112th Congresses)

**WATSON, DIANE.** Democrat; California, 32nd District (107th Congress) and 33rd District (108th–111th Congresses). Elected to the 107th Congress in a June 5, 2001, special election to fill vacancy caused by death of Julian Dixon; reelected to the 108th–111th Congresses (served June 7, 2001–January 3, 2011)

Committee assignments:

- H. Government Reform/Oversight and Government Reform (107th–111th Congresses)
- H. International Relations (107th–109th Congresses)
- H. Foreign Affairs (110th–111th Congresses)

**WATSON COLEMAN, BONNIE.** Democrat; New Jersey, 12th District. Elected to the 114th–115th Congresses (served January 3, 2015–present)

Committee assignments:

- H. Homeland Security (114th–115th Congresses)
- H. Oversight and Government Reform (114th–115th Congresses)

**WILLIAMS, NIKEMA NATASSHA.** Democrat; Georgia, 5th District. Elected to the 117th Congress—present

Committee assignments:

- Financial Services

**WILSON, FREDERICA.** Democrat; Florida, 17th District (112th Congress), 24th District (113th Congress—present). Elected to the 112th–115th Congresses (served January 3, 2011–present)

Committee assignments:

- H. Foreign Affairs (112th Congress)
- H. Science, Space and Technology (112th–113th Congresses)
- H. Education and the Workforce (114th–115th Congresses)
- H. Transportation and Infrastructure (115th Congresses)

# References

#TRUST Black Women. (n.d.). https://trustblackwomen.org/2011-05-10-03-28-12/
publications-a-articles/african-americans-and-abortion-articles/36-african-
american-women-are-for-reproductive-freedom

AP News. (2024, November 13). *2024 Texas election results*. https://apnews.
com/projects/election-results-2024/texas/?r=45900

Apple, R. W. (1991, October 16). Senate confirms Thomas, 52–48, ending week
of bitter battle; "time for healing," judge says. *The New York Times*. https://
www.nytimes.com/1991/10/16/us/thomas-confirmation-senate-confirms-
thomas-52-48-ending-week-bitter-battle-time.html

Barnello, M. A., & Bratton, K. A. (2007). Bridging the gender gap in bill sponsorship. *Legislative Studies Quarterly*, 32(3), 449–474. https://doi.
org/10.3162/036298007781699645

Bash, D. (2021, March 28). Nikema Williams blazes her own trail in the footsteps of history. *CNN Politics*. https://www.cnn.com/2021/03/28/politics/
badass-women-nikema-williams-georgia-voting-rights/index.html

Baumann, R. F., Gawrych, G. W., & Kretchik, W. E. (2024, July 25). *Armed
forces of Bosnia and Herzegovina*. Wikipedia. https://en.wikipedia.org/wiki/
Armed_Forces_of_Bosnia_and_Herzegovina

*BBC News*. (2020, June 9). https://www.bbc.com/news/world-africa-52978780

Beail, L., Bose, M., Burrell, B., Conroy, M., Elder, L., Farrar-Myers, V. A.,
Frederick, B., Goren, L. J., Han, L. C., Heldman, C., Hult, K. M., Knight-
Finley, M., & Pluta, A. (2022). *Madam president: Gender and politics on the
road to the White House*. Lynne Rienner Publishers.

Bernanke, B. S. (2013, July 10). *A century of U.S. Central Banking: Goals,
frameworks, accountability* [Speech]. Board of Governors of the Federal
Reserve System, Washington, DC.

Black Declaration of Independence. (n.d.). [Box 6: Folder 24] *Congressional Black Caucus preliminary inventory*. Moorland-Spingarn Research Center at Howard University in Washington, DC.

Black Law Students Association. (2022, January 31). University of Chicago Law School. https://www.law.uchicago.edu/studentorgs/blsa

Bornemeier, J. (1994, July 30). Waters-king verbal slugfest spills over onto House floor. *Los Angeles Times*. https://www.latimes.com/archives/la-xpm-1994-07-30-mn-21548-story.html

Bridges, B. (2020, November 18). African Americans and college education by the numbers. *UNCF*. https://uncf.org/the-latest/african-americans-and-college-education-by-the-numbers

Budryk, Z. (2020, January 15). Harris calls for judicial nominee freeze during impeachment trial. *The Hill*. https://thehill.com/homenews/senate/478476-harris-calls-for-judicial-nominee-freeze-during-impeachment-trial/

Bush, C. (2021, August 6). Opinion: Rep. Cori Bush: I slept on the Capitol steps because I've been evicted three times in my life. *CNN*. https://www.cnn.com/2021/08/06/opinions/sleep-on-capitol-steps-for-eviction-moratorium-motivation-cori-bush/index.html

California, S. of. (2024, June 17). *Governor Gavin Newsom appoints Laphonza Butler to the U.S. senate*. Governor of California. https://www.gov.ca.gov/2023/10/01/governor-gavin-newsom-appoints-laphonza-butler-senate/

Crabtree, S. (2016, February 3). Bank at center of waters controversy got $12 million bailout despite reviews. *The Hill*. https://thehill.com/homenews/house/70228-bank-at-center-of-waters-controversy-got-12-million-bailout-despite-reviews/

Crenshaw, K. (1991). Mapping the margins: Intersectionality, identity politics, and violence against women of color. Stanford Law Review, 43(6), 1241. https://doi.org/10.2307/1229039

Creswell, J. W. (2014). *A concise introduction to mixed methods research*. Sage Publications.

CREW | Citizens for Responsibility and Ethics in Washington. (2024, November 7). *Reports & investigations—crew: Citizens for responsibility and ethics in Washington*. https://www.citizensforethics.org/reports-and-investigations/?topics=corruption&category=crew-investigations#filterformConfirmation; https://thegrio.com/2021/01/28/hud-secretary-marcia-fudge-confirmation/

Committee on House Administration of the U. S. House of Representatives. (2008). *Black Americans in Congress, 1870-2007*. United States Government Printing Office.

Congressional Record Volume 140, Number 65 (1994, May 23) https://www. govinfo.gov/content/pkg/CREC-1994-05-23/html/CREC-1994-05-23-pt1-PgS24.htm

Correspondence sent from Congressman Espy to CBC Chair Ronald Dellums. (1990, October 5). [Box 1: Folder William Clay], *Ronald V. Dellums Congressional Papers*. Moorland-Spingarn Research Center at Howard University in Washington, DC.

C-SPAN. (1994, July 29). *Whitewater controversy on House floor*. https://www.c-span.org/video/?59115-1%2Fwhitewater-controversy-house-floor

C-SPAN. (2006, February 25). *State of the Black Union 2006: Emerging leaders*. https://www.c-span.org/video/?191199-3%2Fstate-black-union-2006-emerging-leaders

C-SPAN. (2018, September 5) *Exchange between Sen. Harris and Judge Kavanaugh on Mueller investigation*. https://youtu.be/Tsm1GPnlqmU?si=ZCoCDw0uHEudT_3w

C-SPAN. (2020, January 13). *Senator Kamala Harris speaks about President Trump's impeachment trial*. https://www.c-span.org/video/?c4845485%2Fsenator-kamala-harris-speaks-president-trumps-impeachment-trial

C-SPAN. (2024, September 24). House ways and means committee hearing on welfare. https://www.c-span.org/program/public-affairs-event/house-ways-and-means-committee-hearing-on-welfare-accountability/649418

Debenedetti, G., & Damron, W. (2022). *The Long Alliance: The Imperfect Union of Joe Biden and Barack Obama*. Macmillan Audio.

Devine, F. (1998). Class analysis and the stability of class relations. *Sociology*, 32(1), 23–42. https://doi.org/10.1177/0038038598032001003

Diaz, M. (2023, December 15). Veteran homelessness increased by 7.4% in 2023. *VA News*. https://news.va.gov/126913/veteran-homelessness-increased-by-7-4-in-2023/#

Digital, F. (2023, October 23). Leaked audio: Sheila Jackson Lee cusses out staffer in profanity-laced rant. *FOX 26 Houston*. https://www.fox26houston.com/news/sheila-jackson-lee-cusses-out-staffer-in-leaked-audio-recording

DiMartino, D., & Duca, J. V. (2007). The rise and fall of subprime mortgages. *Federal Reserve Bank of Dallas Economic Letter*, 2(11), 1–8.

Dimock, M. (2019, January 17). *Defining generations: Where millennials end and generation Z begins*. Pew Research Center. https://www.pewresearch.org/short-reads/2019/01/17/where-millennials-end-and-generation-z-begins/

DiSalvo, D. (2009). Party factions in Congress. *Congress & the Presidency*, 36(1), 31.

Dowe, P. K. (2020). Resisting marginalization: Black women's political ambition and agency. *PS: Political Science & Politics, 53*(4), 697–702. https://doi.org/10.1017/s1049096520000554

Duca, J. V., Muellbauer, J., & Murphy, A. (2011). House prices and credit constraints: Making sense of the US experience. *The Economic Journal, 121*(552), 533–551. https://doi.org/10.1111/j.1468-0297.2011.02424.x

Else-Quest, N. M., & Hyde, J. S. (2016). Intersectionality in quantitative psychological research: I. Theoretical and epistemological issues. *Psychology of Women Quarterly, 40*(2), 155–170. https://doi.org/10.1177/0361684316629797

EMILYs List. (2023, October 3). *About us.* https://emilyslist.org/about/

Environmental Law Institute. (n.d.). *Eleanor Holmes Norton.* https://www.eli.org/bios/eleanor-holmes-norton

Evers-Hillstrom, K. (2020, January 14). *More money, less transparency: A Decade under Citizens United.* OpenSecrets. https://www.opensecrets.org/news/reports/a-decade-under-citizens-united

Ford, , P. K. (2020). Resisting marginalization: Black women's political ambition and agency. *PS: Political Science & Politics,, 53*(4), 697–702. https://doi.org/10.1017/s1049096520000554

Ford, P. K. (2024). *The radical imagination of black women: Ambition, politics, and power.* Oxford University Press.

Fram, A., & Lemire, J. (2018, May 1). Trump: Why allow immigrants from "shithole countries"? *AP News.* https://apnews.com/article/immigration-north-america-donald-trump-ap-top-news-international-news-fdda2ff0b877416c8ae-1c1a77a3cc425

Fudge, M. (2004, February 14). *City of Warrensville.* About the mayor. https://web.archive.org/web/20070620223902/http://www.cityofwarrensville.com/mayor.htm

Fundraising letter sent to donors from the CBC Chair. (1971, June 18). [Box 82: Folder 2], *Congressional Black Caucus Preliminary Inventory.* Moorland-Spingarn Research Center at Howard University in Washington, DC.

Grant, K. N. (2020). *The great migration and the democratic party: Black voters and the* realignment of American politics in the 20th Century. Temple University Press.

Goldthorpe, J. H. (1998). Rational action theory for sociology. *The British Journal of Sociology, 49*(2), 167–192.

Gore, D. (2017, January 19). Eight years of trolling Obama. *FactCheck.org.* https://www.factcheck.org/2017/01/eight-years-of-trolling-obama/

Govindarao, S. (2024, July 20). U.S. rep. Sheila Jackson Lee is dead at 74. *The Texas Tribune.* https://www.texastribune.org/2024/07/19/sheila-jackson-lee-dies/

Green, E. L., & Cowley, S. (2019, November 28). Broken promises and debt pile up as loan forgiveness goes astray. *New York Times.* https://www.nytimes.com/2019/11/28/us/politics/student-loan-forgiveness.html?auth=login-facebook

Heldman, C., Conroy, M., & Ackerman, A. (2018). *Sex and gender in the 2016 presidential election.* Praeger, an imprint of ABC-CLIO, LLC.

Henderson, N.-M. (2015, January 6). Mia Love joins a group she promised to dismantle. *The Washington Post.* https://www.washingtonpost.com/news/the-fix/wp/2015/01/06/mia-love-joins-the-cbc-the-group-she-vowed-to-dismantle/

The HistoryMakers. (n.d.). *The honorable Eddie Bernice Johnson's biography.* https://www.thehistorymakers.org/biography/honorable-eddie-bernice-johnson

Homelessness and Racial Disparities. National Alliance to End Homelessness. (2025, January 24). https://endhomelessness.org/homelessness-in-america/what-causes-homelessness/inequality/

Hong, P. Y. (2009, January 20). Southern California home prices close out 2008 down 35%. *Los Angeles Times.* https://www.latimes.com/archives/la-xpm-2009-jan-20-fi-housing20-story.html

Howard, J. (2020, June 23). Institutional racism contributes to Covid-19's "double whammy" impact on the Black community, Fauci says. *CNN.* https://www.cnn.com/2020/06/23/health/coronavirus-pandemic-racism-fauci-bn/index.html

Hubler, S. (2022, November 16). Karen Bass becomes first woman elected as Los Angeles mayor. *The New York Times.* https://www.nytimes.com/2022/11/16/us/politics/la-mayor-race-california-caruso-bass.html

Institute for Veterans and Military Families. (2022, February). *Missing perspectives: Black & African Americans in the military—From service to civilian life (2022).* Institute for Veterans and Military Families at Syracuse University. https://surface.syr.edu/ivmf/138/

Jan, T. (2018, March 28). Redlining was banned 50 years ago. It's still hurting minorities today. *Washington Post.* https://www.washingtonpost.com/news/wonk/wp/2018/03/28/redlining-was-banned-50-years-ago-its-still-hurting-minorities-today/

Jan, T. (2021, March 10). Marcia Fudge confirmed as first Black woman to lead HUD in more than 40 years. *The Washington Post.* https://www.washingtonpost.com/business/2021/03/10/hud-secretary-marcia-fudge-confirmation

Johnson, G., Oppenheimer, B. I., & Selin, J. L. (2012). The house as a stepping stone to the Senate: Why do so few African American House members run? *American Journal of Political Science, 56*(2), 387–399. https://doi.org/10.1111/j.1540-5907.2011.00562.x

Jones, J. (2025, January 3). Stacey Plaskett makes waves during House speaker vote with point about voting. *MSNBC.* https://www.msnbc.com/the-reidout/reidout-blog/stacey-plaskett-house-speaker-vote-virgin-islands-rcna186183

Jones, M. (2014). *Knowledge, power, and Black politics: Collected essays*. New York State University Press.

Joseph, E. (2022, January 26). Sheila Cherfilus-McCormick, Congress' newest member, is ready to fight for Haitians. *PBS*. https://www.pbs.org/newshour/politics/sheila-cherfilus-mccormick-floridas-first-haitian-american-in-congress-on-whats-at-stake-in-2022

Kepley, J. (2019, February 21). UC Law SF congratulates Kamala Harris '89: California's next U.S. senator. *UC Law San Francisco (Formerly UC Hastings)*. https://www.uclawsf.edu/2016/11/09/uc-hastings-congratulates-kamala-harris-89-californias-next-u-s-senator/

Kurtz, J. (2024, May 21). Crockett moves to trademark "bleach blonde bad built Butch Body." *The Hill*. https://thehill.com/blogs/in-the-know/4677117-jasmine-crockett-trademark-bleach-blonde-bad-built-butch-body-marjorie-taylor-greene/

Lee, B. (2001, September 23). *Why I opposed the resolution to authorize force*. https://www.sfgate.com/opinion/article/Why-I-opposed-the-resolution-to-authorize-force-2876893.php

Lee, B. (2020, April 15). Rep. Barbara Lee helps introduce legislation to require federal government to collect and release COVID-19 data on race and ethnicity. *Post News Group*. https://www.postnewsgroup.com/rep-barbara-lee-helps-introduce-legislation-to-require-federal-government-to-collect-and-release-covid-19-data-on-race-and-ethnicity/

Lefever, H. G. (1981). "Playing the Dozens": A Mechanism for Social Control. *Phylon (1960-)*, 42(1), 73–85. https://doi.org/10.2307/274886

Livingston, A., & Salhotra, P. (2023, December 31). Former U.S. rep. Eddie Bernice Johnson, Black Democratic Trailblazer, dies at 89. *The Texas Tribune*. https://www.texastribune.org/2023/12/31/texas-eddie-bernice-johnson-dies/

Lewis, T. E., & Nelson, S. J. (2021). Insulated Blackness: The cause for fracture in Black political identity. *Politics, Groups, and Identities*, 10(5), 754–766. https://doi.org/10.1080/21565503.2021.1892783

Lozano, J. A. (2024, July 30). *"She was unrelenting in her leadership," President Biden Remembers US rep. Sheila Jackson Lee in Houston*. The Associated Press. https://www.nbcdfw.com/news/local/texas-news/president-biden-visits-rep-sheila-jackson-lee-houston/3606098/

Lucas, S., & Medhurst, M. J. (eds.). (2009). Words of a century: *The* top 100 American speeches, 1900-1999. Oxford University Press.

Mahoney, P. G. (2018). Deregulation and the subprime crisis. *Virginia Law Review*, 104, 235–300. efaidnbmnnnibpcajpcglclefindmkaj/https://www.virginialawreview.org/wp-content/uploads/2018/04/104VaLRev235.pdf

Meller, N. (1960). Legislative branch research. *The Western Political Quarterly, 13*(1), 131–153.

Miller, B. (2019, December 9). *The continued student loan crisis for Black borrowers*. Center for American Progress. https://cdn.americanprogress.org/content/uploads/2019/11/26071357/Student-Debt-BRIEF.pdf

Moseley Braun, C. (1994). *Current biography, 1994* (p. 378). H.W. Wilson and Company.

Moseley Braun, C. (2024, September 5). *Senate stories: Speech of Carol Moseley Braun (D-IL), July 22, 1993*. U.S. Senate: Speech of Carol Moseley Braun (D-IL), July 22, 1993. https://www.senate.gov/artandhistory/senate-stories/videos/moseley-braun-1993-cspan.htm

Mui, Y. Q. (2012, July 8). For Black Americans, financial damage from subprime implosion is likely to last. *The Washington Post*. https://www.washingtonpost.com/business/economy/for-black-americans-financial-damage-from-subprime-implosion-is-likely-to-last/2012/07/08/gJQAwNmzWW_story.html

Nelson, S. J. (2022). *The congressional Black Caucus: Fifty years of fighting for equality*. Archway Publishing.

Nordgren, S. (1992, July 26). *Carol Moseley-Braun: The unique candidate*. Associated Press.

Page, F. (2024, November 13). *Carrying the torch: Erica Lee Carter takes oath, continues her mother's legacy in Congress*. KTVZ. https://ktvz.com/cnn-regional/2024/11/12/carrying-the-torch-erica-lee-carter-takes-oath-continues-her-mothers-legacy-in-congress/

Palta, R. (2014, March 23). *Calif. attorney general Kamala Harris announces new division to stop ex-prisoners from committing new crimes*. LAist. https://laist.com/news/kpcc-archive/attorney-general-kamala-harris-announces-new-divis

Poletika, N. (2019, January 18). Tired of going to Funerals: The 1972 National Black political convention in Gary. *Belt Magazine, Indiana History Blog*. https://beltmag.com/1972-national-black-political-convention-gary/

Price, E. (2023, July 2). *United executives want to take taxpayer-funded employee paycheck support for themselves. This Texas congresswoman says no*. IAM District 141. https://iam141.org/united-executives-want-to-take-taxpayer-funded-employee-paycheck-support-for-themselves-this-texas-congresswoman-says-no/

Rahal, S., Dickson, D. D., & Hicks, M. (2021, November 5). Former US rep. Barbara-Rose Collins of Detroit dies after bout with covid-19. *The Detroit News*. https://www.detroitnews.com/story/news/local/detroit-city/2021/11/04/barbara-rose-collins-dies-covid-19-congresswoman-city-council-detroit-board-of-education/6290096001/

Ramirez, J. (2018, February 9). Brooklyn mother and daughter's political path was a first for City. *Spectrum News NY1.* https://ny1.com/nyc/brooklyn/news/2018/02/19/black-history-month-clarkes-profile

Ray, R. (2021, March 31). Why are Blacks dying at higher rates from COVID-19? *Bookings Institute.* https://www.brookings.edu/blog/fixgov/2020/04/09/why-are-blacks-dying-at-higher-rates-from-covid-19/

Reuters. (2019, July 11). *Four killed as car bomb targets funeral in Libya's Benghazi: sources.* https://www.reuters.com/article/us-libya-security/four-killed-as-car-bomb-targets-funeral-in-libyas-benghazi-sources-idUSKCN1U61QW/

Ronald Reagan Presidential Foundation & Institute. (n.d.). *Reaganomics: Economic policy and the Reagan Revolution.* https://www.reaganfoundation.org/ronald-reagan/the-presidency/economic-policy/?srsltid=AfmBOoqMmdvwKCMSJPJxpNNZqTIOmWZ-V8HeF-Wxklz_Nf5QfdHc7IX8

Ryan, A. D. (2024, July 12). Hud secretary-designate Marcia fudge eyes racial equity ahead of Confirmation. *TheGrio.* https://thegrio.com/2021/01/28/hud-secretary-marcia-fudge-confirmation/

Santiago, E. (2020, November 23). Monday night marks 8 years since murder of Jordan Davis over Loud Music at Jacksonville gas station. *First Coast Local News.* https://www.firstcoastnews.com/article/news/local/monday-night-marks-8-years-since-murder-of-jordan-davis-over-loud-music-at-jacksonville-gas-station/77-2297d230-84cb-4cdf-bacd-00b583df6648

Sauer, L. M. (2020, July 1). *What is coronavirus?* John Hopkins Medicine. https://www.hopkinsmedicine.org/health/conditions-and-diseases/coronavirus

Saunders, J., Minor, T., Purdy, J., & Baer, M. (2021, May 7). Federal Appeals Court overturns former US rep. Corrine Brown's conviction. *WJXT.* https://www.news4jax.com/news/local/2021/05/06/appeals-court-vacates-former-us-rep-corrine-browns-convictions/

Schaeffer, K. (2023, January 9). *U.S. Congress continues to grow in racial, ethnic diversity.* Pew Research Center. https://www.pewresearch.org/short-reads/2023/01/09/u-s-congress-continues-to-grow-in-racial-ethnic-diversity/

Schlesinger, J. A. (1966). *Ambition and politics: Political careers in the United States.* Rand McNally.

Shames, S. L. (2017). *Out of the running: Why millennials reject political careers and why it matters.* New York University Press.

Shetterly, M. L. (2016). *Hidden figures: The American Dream and the untold story of the black women mathematicians who helped win the space race.* William Morrow.

Shutt, J. (2024, August 9). *Congress limps toward the end of a disappointing session.* Washington State Standard. https://washingtonstatestandard.com/2024/08/08/

congress-limps-toward-the-end-of-a-disappointing-session-with-just-78-laws-to-show/

Smith, S. S. (2010). Race and trust. *Annual Review of Sociology, 36*(1), 453–475. https://doi.org/10.1146/annurev.soc.012809.102526

Soltau, A. (2004, July 21). *New DA claims higher success rate vs. violent felons.* San Francisco Examiner (p. 4). Archived from the original on October 6, 2024.

Star-Telegram, Ft. W. (2021, August 10). Eyes on Texas. *Chicago Tribune.* https://www.chicagotribune.com/1990/08/19/eyes-on-texas/

St. Pierre, M. A. (1991). Reaganomics and its implications for African-American family life. *Journal of Black Studies, 21*(3), 325–340. http://www.jstor.org/stable/2784341

U.S. Senate. (2024, March 12). *Senators who became president.* https://www.senate.gov/senators/SenatorsWhoBecamePresident.htm#:~:text=To%20date%2C%2017%20senators%20have,Senate%20to%20the%20White%20House.

Talladega College. (n.d.). *Talladega College's Civil Rights Garden receives $125K donation: Campus news.* https://www.talladega.edu/news/talladega-colleges-civil-rights-garden-receives-125k-donation/

Taylor, S., Coleman, B., Dyer, J., Tan, S., Nti-Asare, A., & Sheppard, V. B. (2022, August 10). *Civil rights attorney Jasmine Crockett is making waves as a Texas state representative.* Darling Magazine. https://darlingmagazine.org/interview-with-lawyer-jasmine-crockett/

Tester, H. (2024, February 21). Black history month: Dana Dorsey came to Miami, became a millionaire. *CBS News.* https://www.cbsnews.com/miami/news/black-history-month-dana-dorsey-came-to-miami-became-a-millionaire/

Tie, Y. C., Birks, M., & Francis, K. (2019). Grounded theory research: A design framework for novice researchers. *Sage Open Medicine, 7,* 108.USAFacts. (2023, March 28). *Four Senate campaigns financed over $500 million. Where did that money come from?* https://usafacts.org/articles/four-2022-senate-campaigns-financed-over-500-million-where-did-that-money-come-from/

U.S. Bureau of Labor Statistics. (n.d.). *Labor Force Statistics from the Current Population Survey Unemployment Rate—Black or African American.* U.S. Bureau of Labor Statistics. https://data.bls.gov/pdq/SurveyOutputServlet

U.S. Department of Commerce, National Oceanic and Atmospheric Administration, & National Weather Service. (2022, September 7). *Hurricane Dennis—July 10, 2005.* National Weather Service. https://www.weather.gov/mob/dennis

Wagner, M., Mahtani, M., Macaya, M., Rocha, V., & III, F. A. (2021, June 18). Biden signs Juneteenth Bill. *CNN Politics | CNN.* https://www.cnn.com/politics/live-news/biden-signs-juneteenth-bill/index.html

Waters, M. (2008, March 26). *Congresswoman Waters receives prestigious award in South Africa.* https://waters.house.gov/media-center/press-releases/congresswoman-waters-receives-prestigious-award-south-africa

Wines, M. (1994, December 8) Republicans seek sweeping changes in House's rules. *The New York Times.* https://www.nytimes.com/1994/12/08/us/republicans-seek-sweeping-changes-in-house-s-rules.html.

White House History. (2024, November 14). *The Presidents timeline.* https://www.whitehousehistory.org/the-presidents-timeline

White, J. B. (2021, September 27). *Bass officially launches Los Angeles mayoral run.* Politico. https://www.politico.com/states/california/story/2021/09/27/bass-officially-launches-los-angeles-mayoral-run-1391456

Who I Am, (2019, March 22). *Congressional Black Caucus Foundation* [video]. https://youtu.be/nWDS9j1GVCg

Wright Austin, S. D., & Ford, P. K. (2023). *Political black girl magic: The elections and governance of black female mayors.* Temple University Press.

Yardley, W. (2013, February 7). Cardiss Collins, fighter in Congress for Equality and the poor, dies at 81. *The New York Times.* https://www.nytimes.com/2013/02/08/us/politics/cardiss-collins-illinois-congresswoman-dies-at-81.html

# Index

# Author Bio

**Dr. Sherice Janaye Nelson** is an accomplished political scientist, author, and an assistant professor at Southern University and A&M College. Her scholarly work focuses on Black politics, the African Diaspora, and public policy, with a particular emphasis on data-driven research that amplifies the voices and experiences of Black communities.

She serves as the director of the Jewel Limar Prestage Public Policy, Polling, and Research Center at Southern University, where she leads mixed-methods research initiatives designed to tell the nuanced stories of Black Americans through rigorous qualitative and quantitative inquiry.

Dr. Nelson earned her PhD in Political Science from Howard University, with a specialization in Black Politics and International Relations. A proud HBCU alumna, she holds a Master of Public Administration from the University of the District of Columbia and a dual degree in History and English from Stillman College.

Through her writing, teaching, and research, Dr. Sherice Janaye Nelson continues to shape the field of Black political thought and public policy with a bold, data-informed, and socially responsive approach.

www.ingramcontent.com/pod-product-compliance
Lightning Source LLC
Chambersburg PA
CBHW052114030426
42335CB00025B/2972